Testing with JUnit

Master high-quality software development driven
by unit tests

Frank Appel

BIRMINGHAM - MUMBAI

Testing with JUnit

First published: August 2015

Production reference: 1240815

Published by Packt Publishing Ltd.
Livery Place
35 Livery Street
Birmingham B3 2PB, UK.

ISBN 978-1-78216-660-3

www.packtpub.com

Credits

Author
Frank Appel

Reviewers
Stefan Birkner

Jose Muanis Castro

John Piasetzki

Acquisition Editor
Sonali Vernekar

Content Development Editor
Merwyn D'souza

Technical Editor
Humera Shaikh

Copy Editors
Sarang Chari

Sonia Mathur

Project Coordinator
Nikhil Nair

Proofreader
Safis Editing

Indexer
Monica Ajmera Mehta

Graphics
Jason Monteiro

Production Coordinator
Nilesh R. Mohite

Cover Work
Nilesh R. Mohite

About the Author

Frank Appel is a stalwart of agile methods and test-driven development in particular. He has over 2 decades of experience as a freelancer and understands software development as a type of craftsmanship. Having adopted the *test first* approach over a decade ago, he applies unit testing to all kinds of Java-based systems and arbitrary team constellations. He serves as a mentor, provides training, and blogs about these topics at `codeaffine.com`.

I'd like to thank the reviewers, John Piasetzki, Stefan Birkner, and Jose Muanis Castro, and the editors, Sonali Vernekar, Merwyn D'souza, and Humera Shaikh, who spent time and effort to point out my errors, omissions, and sometimes unintelligible writing. In particular, I would like to thank my friend Holger Staudacher, who helped in the reviewing process of the book.

Thanks to all of you for your valuable input and support!

About the Reviewers

Stefan Birkner has a passion for software development. He has a strong preference for beautiful code, tests, and deployment automation. Stefan is a contributor to JUnit and maintains a few other libraries.

Jose Muanis Castro holds a degree in information systems. Originally from the sunny Rio de Janeiro, he now lives in Brooklyn with his wife and kids. At The New York Times, he works with recommendation systems on the personalization team. Previously, he worked on CMS and publishing platforms at `Globo.com` in Brazil.

Jose is a seasoned engineer with hands-on experience in several languages. He's passionate about continuous improvement, agile methods, and lean processes. With a lot of experience in automation, from testing to deploying, he constantly switches hats between development and operations. When he's not coding, he enjoys riding around on his bike. He was a reviewer on the 2014 book, *Mastering Unit Testing Using Mockito and JUnit, Packt Publishing*. His Twitter handle is `@muanis`.

I'm thankful to my wife, Márcia, and my kids, Vitoria and Rafael, for understanding that I couldn't be there sometimes when I was reviewing this book.

John Piasetzki has over 15 years of professional experience as a software developer. He started out doing programming jobs when he was young and obtained a bachelor of science degree in computer engineering. John was fortunate enough to get his start in programming by contributing to WordPress. He continued by working at IBM on WebSphere while getting his degree. Since then, he has moved on to smaller projects. John has worked with technologies such as Python, Ruby, and most recently, AngularJS. He's currently working as a software developer at OANDA, a foreign exchange company.

www.PacktPub.com

Support files, eBooks, discount offers, and more

For support files and downloads related to your book, please visit www.PacktPub.com.

Did you know that Packt offers eBook versions of every book published, with PDF and ePub files available? You can upgrade to the eBook version at www.PacktPub.com and as a print book customer, you are entitled to a discount on the eBook copy. Get in touch with us at service@packtpub.com for more details.

At www.PacktPub.com, you can also read a collection of free technical articles, sign up for a range of free newsletters and receive exclusive discounts and offers on Packt books and eBooks.

https://www2.packtpub.com/books/subscription/packtlib

Do you need instant solutions to your IT questions? PacktLib is Packt's online digital book library. Here, you can search, access, and read Packt's entire library of books.

Why subscribe?

- Fully searchable across every book published by Packt
- Copy and paste, print, and bookmark content
- On demand and accessible via a web browser

Free access for Packt account holders

If you have an account with Packt at www.PacktPub.com, you can use this to access PacktLib today and view 9 entirely free books. Simply use your login credentials for immediate access.

Table of Contents

Preface

Testing with JUnit is a skill that presents much harder challenges than you might expect at first sight. This is because, despite its temptingly simple API, the tool plays ball with profound and well-conceived concepts. Hence, it's important to acquire a deep understanding of the underlying principles and practices. This avoids ending up in gridlocked development due to messed-up production and testing code.

Mastering high-quality software development driven by unit tests is about following well-attuned patterns and methods as a matter of routine rather, than reinventing the wheel on a daily basis. If you have a good perception of the conceptual requirements and a wide-ranging arsenal of solution approaches, they will empower you to continuously deliver code, which achieves excellent ratings with respect to the usual quality metrics out of the box.

To impart these capabilities, this book provides you with a well-thought-out, step-by-step tutorial. Foundations and essential techniques are elaborated, guided by a golden thread along the development demands of a practically relevant sample application. The chapters and sections are built on one another, each starting with in-depth considerations about the current topic's problem domain and concluding with an introduction to and discussion of the available solution strategies.

At the same time, it's taken care that all thoughts are backed up by illustrative images and expressive listings supplemented by adequate walkthroughs. For the best possible understanding, the complete source code of the book's example app is hosted at `https://github.com/fappel/Testing-with-JUnit`. This allows you to comprehend the various aspects of JUnit testing from within a more complex development context and facilitates an exchange of ideas using the repository's issue tracker.

What this book covers

Chapter 1, Getting Started, opens with a motivational section about the benefits of JUnit testing and warms up with a short coverage of the toolchain used throughout the book. After these preliminaries, the example project is kicked off, and writing the first unit test offers the opportunity to introduce the basics of the test-driven development paradigm.

Chapter 2, Writing Well-structured Tests, explains why the four fundamental phases' test pattern is perfectly suited to test a unit's behavior. It elaborates on several fixture initialization strategies, shows how to deduce what to test, and concludes by elucidating different test-naming conventions.

Chapter 3, Developing Independently Testable Units, shows you how to decompose big requirements into small and separately testable components and illustrates the impact of collaboration dependencies on testing efforts. It explains the importance of test isolation and demonstrates the use of test doubles to achieve it.

Chapter 4, Testing Exceptional Flow, discusses the pros and cons of various exception capture and verification techniques. Additionally, it explains the meaning of the *fail fast* strategy and outlines how it intertwines with tests on particular boundary conditions.

Chapter 5, Using Runners for Particular Testing Purposes, presents JUnit's pluggable test processor architecture that allows us to adjust test execution to highly diverse demands. It covers how to write custom runners and introduces several useful areas of application.

Chapter 6, Reducing Boilerplate with JUnit Rules, unveils the test interception mechanism behind the rule concept, which allows you to provide powerful, test-related helper classes. After deepening the knowledge by writing a sample extension, the chapter continues with the tools' built-in utilities and concludes by inspecting useful third-party vendor offerings.

Chapter 7, Improving Readability with Custom Assertions, teaches the writing of concise verifications that reveal the expected outcome of a test clearly. It shows how domain-specific assertions help you to improve readability and discusses the assets and drawbacks of the built-in mechanisms, Hamcrest and AssertJ.

Chapter 8, Running Tests Automatically within a CI Build, concludes the example project with important considerations of test-related architectural aspects. Finally, it rounds out the book by giving an introduction to continuous integration, which is an excellent brief of the *test first* approach and establishes short feedback cycles efficiently by automation.

Appendix, *References*, lists all the bibliographic references used throughout the chapters of this book.

What you need for this book

For better understanding and deepening of the knowledge acquired, it's advisable to comprehend the examples within a local workspace on your computer. As JUnit is written in Java, the most important thing you need is Java Development Kit. The sample code requires at least Java 8, which can be downloaded from `http://www.oracle.com/technetwork/java/index.html`.

Although it's possible to compile and run the listings from the command line, the book assumes you're working with a Java IDE, such as Eclipse (`http://www.eclipse.org/`), IntelliJ IDEA (`https://www.jetbrains.com/idea/`) or NetBeans (`https://netbeans.org/`). The sample application was developed using Eclipse and so are the screenshots.

As mentioned in the preceding paragraph, the book's code sources are hosted at GitHub, so you can clone your local copy using Git (`https://git-scm.com/`). The chapter and sample app projects are based on Maven (`https://maven.apache.org/`) with respect to their structure and dependency management, which makes it easy to get the sample solutions up and running. This allows a thorough live inspection and debugging of passages that are not fully understood.

Due to this availability of comprehensive sources, the listings in the chapters are stripped down using static imports wherever appropriate or use ellipses to denote a class that has content unrelated to the topic. This helps you to keep the snippets small and focus on the important stuff.

Apart from that, in the course of the book, several Java libraries are introduced. They can all be declared as Maven dependencies and can be downloaded automatically from the publicly available Maven Central Repository (`http://search.maven.org/`). For some examples, you can refer to the pom.xml files of the sample application. An overview of the testing toolset is given in *Chapter 1*, *Getting Started*.

Who this book is for

No matter what your specific background as a Java developer is, whether you're simply interested in building up a safety net to reduce the regression of your desktop application or in improving your server-side reliability based on robust and reusable components, unit testing is the way to go. This book provides you with a comprehensive, but concise, entrance, advancing your knowledge step-wise, to a professional level.

Conventions

In this book, you will find a number of text styles that distinguish between different kinds of information. Here are some examples of these styles and an explanation of their meaning.

Code words in text, database table names, folder names, filenames, file extensions, pathnames, dummy URLs, user input, and Twitter handles are shown as follows: "As a result, a test case was a compound of various methods called testFoo, testBar, and so on."

A block of code is set as follows:

```
private final static int NEW_FETCH_COUNT
  = Timeline.DEFAULT_FETCH_COUNT + 1;

@Test
public void setFetchCount() {
  // (1) setup (arrange, build)
  Timeline timeline = new Timeline();

  // (2) exercise (act, operate)
  timeline.setFetchCount( NEW_FETCH_COUNT );

  // (3) verify (assert, check)
  assertEquals( NEW_FETCH_COUNT, timeline.getFetchCount() );
}
```

When we wish to draw your attention to a particular part of a code block, the relevant lines or items are set in bold:

```
private ItemProvider itemProvider;
private Timeline timeline;

@Before
public void setUp() {
  itemProvider = ???
  timeline = new Timeline( itemProvider );
}
```

Any command-line input or output is written as follows:

```
mvn clean test
```

New terms and **important words** are shown in bold like this: "Changing code without changing its behavior is called **refactoring**."

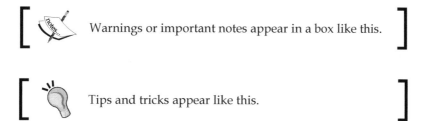

Warnings or important notes appear in a box like this.

Tips and tricks appear like this.

Reader feedback

Feedback from our readers is always welcome. Let us know what you think about this book—what you liked or disliked. Reader feedback is important for us as it helps us develop titles that you will really get the most out of.

To send us general feedback, simply e-mail feedback@packtpub.com, and mention the book's title in the subject of your message.

If there is a topic that you have expertise in and you are interested in either writing or contributing to a book, see our author guide at www.packtpub.com/authors.

Customer support

Now that you are the proud owner of a Packt book, we have a number of things to help you to get the most from your purchase.

Downloading the example code

You can download the example code files from your account at http://www.packtpub.com for all the Packt Publishing books you have purchased. If you purchased this book elsewhere, you can visit http://www.packtpub.com/support and register to have the files e-mailed directly to you.

Downloading the color images of this book

We also provide you with a PDF file that has color images of the screenshots/
diagrams used in this book. The color images will help you better understand the
changes in the output. You can download this file from: `https://www.packtpub.`
`com/sites/default/files/downloads/6603OS_Graphics.pdf`.

Errata

Although we have taken every care to ensure the accuracy of our content, mistakes
do happen. If you find a mistake in one of our books—maybe a mistake in the text or
the code—we would be grateful if you could report this to us. By doing so, you can
save other readers from frustration and help us improve subsequent versions of this
book. If you find any errata, please report them by visiting `http://www.packtpub.`
`com/submit-errata`, selecting your book, clicking on the **Errata Submission Form**
link, and entering the details of your errata. Once your errata are verified, your
submission will be accepted and the errata will be uploaded to our website or added
to any list of existing errata under the Errata section of that title.

To view the previously submitted errata, go to `https://www.packtpub.com/books/`
`content/support` and enter the name of the book in the search field. The required
information will appear under the **Errata** section.

Piracy

Piracy of copyrighted material on the Internet is an ongoing problem across all
media. At Packt, we take the protection of our copyright and licenses very seriously.
If you come across any illegal copies of our works in any form on the Internet, please
provide us with the location address or website name immediately so that we can
pursue a remedy.

Please contact us at `copyright@packtpub.com` with a link to the suspected
pirated material.

We appreciate your help in protecting our authors and our ability to bring you
valuable content.

Questions

If you have a problem with any aspect of this book, you can contact us at
`questions@packtpub.com`, and we will do our best to address the problem.

1
Getting Started

Accomplishing the evolving objectives of a software project in time and budget on a long-term basis is a difficult undertaking. In this opening chapter, we're going to explain why unit testing can play a vital role in meeting these demands. We'll illustrate the positive influence on the defect rate, code quality, development pace, specification density, and team morale. All that makes it worthwhile to acquire a broad understanding of the various testing techniques. To get started, you'll learn to arrange our tool set around JUnit and organize our project infrastructure properly. You'll be familiarized with the definition of unit tests and the basics of test-driven development. This will prepare us for the following chapters, where you'll come to know about more advanced testing practices.

- Why you should busy yourself with unit tests
- Setting the table
- Serving the starter

Why you should busy yourself with unit tests

Since you are reading this, you likely have a reason to consider unit testing as an additional development skill to learn. Whether you are motivated by personal interest or driven by external stimulus, you probably wonder if it will be worth the effort. But properly applied unit testing is perhaps the most important technique the agile world has to offer. A well-written test suite is usually half the battle for a successful development process, and the following section will explain why.

Reducing the defect rate

The most obvious reason to write unit tests is to build up a safety net to guard your software from regression. There are various grounds for changing the existing code, whether it be to fix a bug or to add supplemental functionality. But understanding every aspect of the code you are about to change is difficult to achieve. So, a new bug sneaks in easily. And it might take a while before it gets noticed.

Think of a method returning some kind of sorted list that works as expected. Due to additional requirements, such as filtering the result, a developer changes the existing code. Inadvertently, these changes introduce a bug that only surfaces under rare circumstances. Hence, simple sanity tests may not reveal any problems and the developer feels confident to check in the new version. If the company is lucky, the problem will be detected by the quality assurance team, but chances are that it slips through to the customer. Boom!

This is because it's hardly possible to check all corner cases of a nontrivial software from a user's point of view, let alone if done manually. Besides an annoyed customer, this leads to a costly turnaround consisting of, for example, filing a bug report, reproducing and debugging the problem, scheduling it for repair, implementing the fix, testing, delivering, and, finally, deploying the corrected version. But who will guarantee that the new version won't introduce another regression?

Sounds scary? It is! I have seen teams that were barely able to deliver new functionality as they were about to drown in a flood of bugs. And hot fixes produced to resolve blocking situations on the customer side introduced additional regression all the time. Sounds familiar? Then, it might be time for a change.

Good unit tests can be written with a small development overhead and verify, in particular, all the corner case behavior of a component. Thus, the developer's said mistake would have been captured by a test. At the earliest possible point in time and at the lowest possible price. But humans make mistakes: what if a corner case is overlooked and a bug turns up? Even then, you are better off because fixing the issue sustainably means simply writing an additional test that reproduces the problem by a failing verification. Change the code until all tests pass and you get rid of the fault forever.

Improving the code quality

The influence a consistent testing approach will have on the code quality is less apparent. Once you have a safety net in place, changing the existing code to make it more readable, and hence easier to enhance, isn't risky anymore. If you are introducing a regression, your tests will tell you immediately. So, the code morphs from a *never touch a running system* shrine to a lively *change embracing* place.

Matured test-first practices will implicitly improve your code with respect to most of the common quality metrics. Testing first is geared to produce small, coherent, and loosely coupled components combined with a high coverage and verification of the component's behavior. The production of *clean code* is an inherent step of the test-driven development mantra explained further ahead.

The following image shows two screenshots of measurements taken from a small, real-world project of the **Xiliary** GitHub repository (`https://github.com/fappel/xiliary`). Developed completely driven by tests, we couldn't care less about the project's metrics before writing this chapter. But not very surprisingly, the numbers look quite okay.

 Don't worry if you're not familiar with the meaning of the metrics. All you need to know at the moment is that they would appear in red if exceeding the tool's default thresholds.

So, in case you wonder about the three red spots with low coverage numbers, note that two of those classes are covered by particular integration tests as they are adapters to third-party functionality (a more detailed explanation of integration tests follows in the upcoming *Understanding the nature of a unit test* section). The remaining class is at an experimental or prototypical stage and will be replaced in the future.

Note that we'll deepen our knowledge of code coverage in *Chapter 2, Writing Well-structured Tests,* and in *Chapter 8, Running Tests Automatically within a CI Build.*

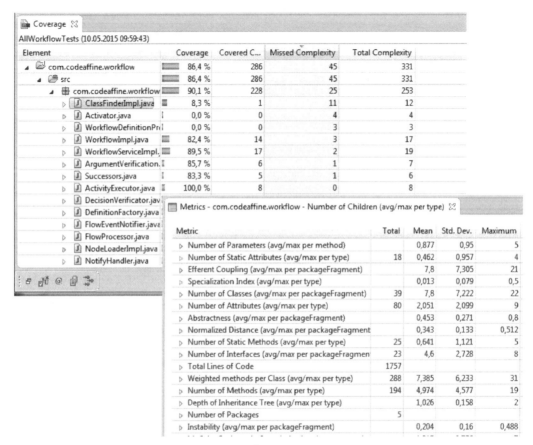

Metrics of a TDD project

Programs built on good code quality stand out from systems that merely run, because they are easier to maintain and usually impress with a higher feature evolution rate.

Increasing the development pace

At first glance, the math seems to be simple. Writing additional testing code means more work, which consumes more time, which leads to lower development speed. Right? But would you like to drive a car whose individual parts did not undergo thorough quality assurance? And what would be gained if the car had to spend most of its lifetime in the service shop rather than on the road, let alone the possibility of a life-threatening accident?

The initial production speed might be high, but the overall outcome would be poor and might ruin the car manufacturer in the end. It is not that much different with the development of nontrivial software systems. We elaborated already on the costs of bugs that manage to sneak through to the customer. So, it is a naïve assessment calculating development speed like that.

As a developer, you stand between two contradictory goals: on the one hand, you have to be quick on the draw to meet your deadlines. On the other hand, you must not commit too many sins to be able to also meet *subsequent* deadlines. The term sin refers to work that should be done before a particular job can be considered complete or proper. This is also denoted as **technical debt**, *[TECDEP]*. And here comes the catch. Keeping the balance often does not work out, and once the technical debt gets too high, the system collapses. From that point in time, you won't meet any deadlines again.

So, yes, writing tests causes an overhead. But if done well, it ensures that subsequent deadlines are not endangered by technical debt. The development pace might be initially at a slightly lower rate with testing, but it won't decrease and is, therefore, higher when watching the overall picture.

By the way, if you know your tools and techniques, the overhead isn't that much at all. At least, I am usually not hired for being particularly slow. When you think of it, running a component's unit tests is done in the time of a wink. On the flip side, checking its behavior manually involves launching the application, clicking to the point where your code actually gets involved, and after that, you click and type yourself again through certain scenarios you consider important. Does the latter sound like an efficient modus operandi?

Enhancing the specification density

A good test suite at hand can be an additional source of information about what your system components are really capable of and one that doesn't outdate unlike design docs, which usually do. Of course, this is a kind of low-level specification that only a developer is apt to write. But if done well, a test's name tells you about the functionality under test with respect to specific initial conditions and the test's verifications about the expected outcome produced by the execution of this functionality.

This way, a developer who is about to change an existing component will always have a chance to check against the accompanying tests to understand what a component is really all about. So, the truth is in the tests! But this underscores that tests have to be treated as first-class citizens and have to be written and adjusted with care. A poorly written test might confuse a programmer and hinder the progressing rate significantly.

Boosting confidence and courage

Everybody likes to be in a winning team. But once you are stuck in a bug trail longer than the Great Wall of China and a technical debt higher than Mount Everest, fear creeps in. At that time, the implementation of new features can cause avalanches of lateral damage and developers get reluctant to changes. What follow are debates about consolidation phases or even rewriting large parts of the system from scratch before they dare to think about new functionality. Of course, this is an economic horror scenario from the management's point of view, and that's how the development team member's confidence and courage say good bye.

Again, this does not happen as easily with a team that has build its software upon components backed up with well-written unit tests. We learned earlier why unit tested systems neither have many bugs nor too much technical debt. Introducing additional functionality is possible without expecting too much lateral damage since the existing tests beware of regressions. Combined with module-spanning integration tests, you get a rock-solid foundation in which developers learn to trust.

I have seen more than once how restructuring requirements of nontrivial systems were achieved without doing any harm to dependent components. All that was necessary was to take care not to break existing tests and cover changed code passages with new or adjusted tests. So, if you are unluckily more or less familiar with some of the scenarios described in this section, you should read on and learn how to get confidence and courage back in your team.

Setting the table

This book is based on a hands-on example that will guide us through the essential concepts and programming techniques of unit testing. For a sustainable learning experience, feel encouraged to elaborate and complete the various code snippets in your own working environment. Hence, here comes a short introduction of the most important tools and the workspace organization used while programming the sample.

Choosing the ingredients

As the book's title implies, the main tool this is all about is **JUnit** (`http://www.junit.org`). It is probably the most popular testing framework for developers within the Java world. Its first version was written by Kent Beck and Eric Gamma on a flight from Zurich to OOPSLA 1997 in Atlanta, *[FOWL06]*. Since then, it has evolved by adapting to changing language constructs, and quite a few supplemental libraries have emerged.

Java IDEs provide a UI and build path entries to compile, launch, and evaluate JUnit tests. Build tools, such as Ant, Maven, and Gradle, support test integration out of the box. When it comes to IDEs, the example screenshots in this book are captured using **Eclipse** (`http://www.eclipse.org/`). However, we do not rely on any Eclipse-specific features, which should make it easy to reproduce the results in your favorite IDE too.

In general, we use **Maven** (`https://maven.apache.org/`) for dependency management of the libraries mentioned next, which means that they can be retrieved from the **Maven Central Repository** (`http://search.maven.org/`). But if you clone the book's GitHub repository (`https://github.com/fappel/Testing-with-JUnit`), you will find a separate folder for each chapter, providing a complete project configuration with all dependencies and sources. This means navigating to this directory and using the `'mvn test'` Maven command should enable you to compile and run the given examples easily. Let's finish this section with an introduction of the more important utilities we'll be using in the course of the book.

Chapter 3, Developing Independently Testable Units, covers the sense and purpose of the various test double patterns. It is no wonder that there are tools that simplify test double creation significantly. Usually, they are summarized under the term mock frameworks. The examples are based on **Mockito** (`http://mockito.org`), which suits very well to building up clean and readable test structures.

There are several libraries that claim to improve your daily testing work. *Chapter 5, Using Runners for Particular Testing Purposes*, will introduce **JUnitParams** (`http://pragmatists.github.io/JUnitParams/`) and **Burst** (`https://github.com/square/burst`) as alternatives to writing parameterized tests. *Chapter 7, Improving Readability with Custom Assertions*, will compare the two verification tools **Hamcrest** (`http://hamcrest.org/`) and **AssertJ** (`http://assertj.org`).

Automated tests are only valuable if they are executed often. Because of this, they are usually an inherent part of each project's continuous integration build. Hence, *Chapter 8, Running Tests Automatically within a CI Build*, will show how to create a basic build with Maven and introduce the value of code coverage reports with **JaCoCo** (`http://www.eclemma.org/jacoco/`).

Organizing your code

In the beginning, one of the more profane-looking questions you have to agree upon within your team is where to put the test code. The usual convention is to keep unit tests in classes with the same name as the class under test, but post- or prefixed with an extension `Test` or such like. Thus, a test case for the `Foo` class might be named `FooTest`.

Based on the description of *Hunt/Thomas*, *[HUTH03]*, of different project structuring types, the simplest approach would be to put our test into the same directory where the production code resides, as shown in the following diagram:

```
com/
|_____bar/
         |_____Foo
         |_____FooTest
```

A single-source tree with the same package

We usually don't want to break the encapsulation of our classes for testing purposes, which shouldn't be necessary in most cases anyway. But as always, there are exceptions to the rule, and before leaving a functionality untested, it's probably better to open up the visibility a bit. The preceding code organization provides the advantage that, in such rare cases, one can make use of the package member access the Java language offers.

Members or methods without visibility modifiers, such as public, protected, and private, are only accessible from classes within the same package. A test case that resides in the same package can use such members, while encapsulation still shields them from classes outside the package, even if such classes would extend the type under test.

Unfortunately, putting tests into the same directory as the production code has a great disadvantage too. When packages grow, the test cases are perceived soon as clutter and lead to confusion when looking at the package's content. Because of this, another possibility is to have particular test subpackages, as shown here:

```
com/
|_____bar/
       |_____Foo
       |_____test/
               |_____FooTest
```

Single-source tree with a separate test package

However, using this structure, we give up the package member access. But how can we achieve a better separation of production and testing code without loosing this capability? The answer is to introduce a parallel source tree for test classes, as shown here:

```
src/
|_____com/
       |_____bar/
              |_____Foo
test/
|_____com/
       |_____bar/
              |_____FooTest
```

A parallel-source tree

To make this work, it is important that the root of both trees are part of the compiler's CLASSPATH settings. Luckily, you usually do not have to put much effort in this organization as it is the most common one and gets set up automatically, for example, if you use Maven archetypes to create your projects. Examples in this book assume this structure.

Last but not least, it is possible to enhance the parallel tree concept even further. A far-reaching separation can be achieved by putting tests in their own source code project. The advantage of this strategy is the ability to use different compiler error/warning settings for test and production code. This is useful, for example, if you decide to avoid auto-boxing in your components but feel it would make test code overly verbose when working with primitives. With project-specific settings, you can have hard compiler errors in production code without having the same restriction in tests.

```
com.bar.project/
|____src/
        |____com/
                |____bar/
                        |_____Foo
com.bar.project.test/
|____test/
        |____com/
                |____bar/
                        |_____FooTest
```

Parallel-source tree with separate test project

Whatever organization style you may choose, make sure that all team members use the same one. It will be very confusing and hardly maintainable, if the different concepts get mixed up. Now that the preliminaries are done, we are ready for action.

Serving the starter

To reach as much practical relevance as possible, this book shows how to implement a real-world scenario driven by unit tests. This way of proceeding allows us to explain the various concepts and techniques under the light of a coherent requirement. Thus, we kick off with a modest specification of what our example application will be all about. However, before finally descending into the depths of development practices, we will go ahead and clarify the basic characteristics of unit testing and test-first practices in dedicated sections.

Introducing the example app

Let's assume that we have to write a simple timeline component as it is known from the various social networks, such as Twitter, Google+, Facebook, and the like. To make things a bit more interesting, the application has to run on different platforms (desktop, browser, and mobile) and allow the display of content from arbitrary sources. The wireframe in the following image gives an impression of the individual functional requirements of our timeline:

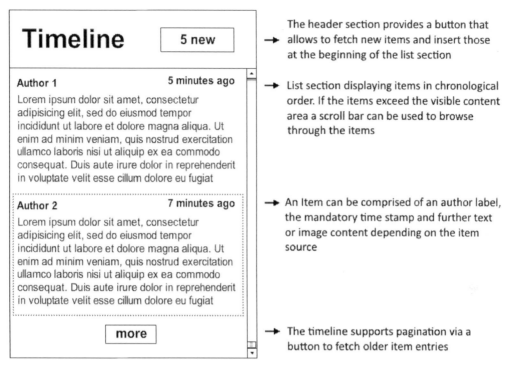

The header section provides a button that allows to fetch new items and insert those at the beginning of the list section

List section displaying items in chronological order. If the items exceed the visible content area a scroll bar can be used to browse through the items

An Item can be comprised of an author label, the mandatory time stamp and further text or image content depending on the item source

The timeline supports pagination via a button to fetch older item entries

Timeline wireframe

The header contains a label indicating the source of the items displayed in the list under it. It also notifies the user if newer entries are available and allows the them to fetch and insert them at the top.

The list section is a sequence of chronologically ordered items, which can be browsed by a scrollbar. The component should allow us to load its entries page-wise. This means that it shows a maximum of, let's say, ten entries. If scrolling reaches the last one, the next ten items can be fetched from the provider. The newly loaded entries are added and the scrollbar is adjusted accordingly. To keep things in scope, a push button for manual fetching will be sufficient here.

An item type, in turn, comprises several text or image attributes that compose an entry's content. Note that the timestamp is considered mandatory as it is needed for chronological ordering. Apart from that, the depiction should be undetermined by the component itself and depend on the type of the underlying information source.

This means that a Twitter feed probably provides a different information structure than the commits of a branch in a Git repository. The following image shows what the running applications will look like. The JUnit items shown are commits taken from the master branch of the tool's project repository at GitHub.

Given the application description, it is important to note that the following chapters will focus on the unit testing aspects of the development process to keep the book on target. But this immediately raises the question: what exactly is a unit test?

Understanding the nature of a unit test

A unit test is basically a piece of code written by a developer to verify that another piece code—usually the implementation of a feature—works correctly. In this context, a unit identifies a very small, specific area of *behavior* and not the implementing code itself. If we regard *adding an item to our timeline* as a functional feature for example, appropriate tests would ensure that the item list grows by one and that the new item gets inserted at the right chronological position.

Yet, there is more to it than meets the eye. Unit tests are restricted to that code for which the developer is responsible. Consider using a third-party library that relies on external resources. Tests would implicitly run against that third-party code. In case one of the external resources is not available, a test could fail although there might be nothing wrong with the developer's code. Furthermore, set up could get painstaking, and due to the invocation time of external resources, execution would get slow.

But we want our unit tests to be very fast because we intend to run them all as often as possible without impeding the pace of development. By doing so, we receive immediate feedback about busting a low-level functionality. This puts us in the position to detect and correct a problem as it evolves and avoid expensive quality assurance cycles.

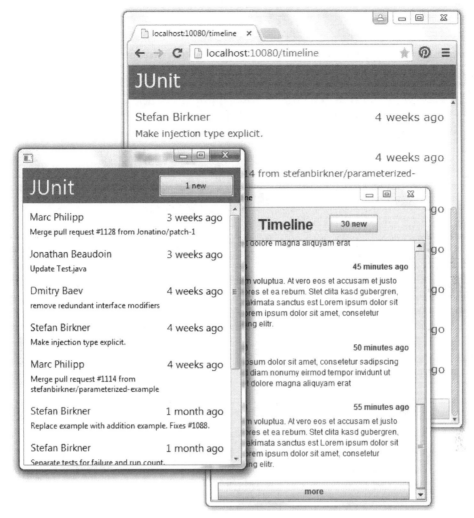

Different timeline UIs

As the book progresses, we will see how to deal with the integration of third-party code properly. The usual strategy is to create an abstraction of the problematic component. This way, it can be replaced by a stand-in that is under the control of the developer. Nevertheless, it is important to verify that the real implementation works as expected. Tests that cope with this task are called **integration** tests. Integration tests check the functionality on a more coarse-grained level and focus on the correct transition of component boundaries.

Having said all this, it is clear that testing a software system from the client's point of view to verify formal specifications does not belong to unit testing either. Such tests simulate user behavior and verify the system as a whole. They usually require a significant amount of time for execution. These kinds of tests are called **acceptance** or **end-to-end** tests.

Another way to look at unit tests is as an accompanying specification of the code under test, comparable to the dispatch note of a cogwheel, which tells **Quality Assurance (QA)** what key figures this piece of work should meet. But due to the nature of the software, no one but the developer is apt to write such low-level specifications. Thus, automated tests become an important source of information about the intended behavior of a unit and one that does not become outdated as easily as documentation.

 We'll elaborate on this thought in *Chapter 2, Writing Well-structured Tests.*

Now that we've heard so much about the nature of unit tests, it's about time to write the first one by ourselves!

Writing the first test

"A journey of a thousand miles begins with a single step."

– Lao Tzu

Unit tests written with JUnit are grouped by plain Java classes, each of which is called a **test case**. A single test case specifies the behavior of a low-level component normally represented by a class. Following the metaphor of the accompanying specification, we can begin the development of our timeline example as follows:

```
public class TimelineTest {
}
```

The test class expresses the intent to develop the a component `Timeline`, which *Meszaros, [MESZ07],* would denote as **system under test (SUT)**. And applying a common naming pattern, the component's name is complemented by the suffix `Test`. But what is the next logical step? What should be tested first? And how do we create an executable test anyway?

Usually, it is a good idea to start with the **happy path**, which is the normal path of execution and, ideally, the general business use case. Consider that we expect fetch-count to be an attribute of our timeline component. The value configures how many items will be fetched at once from an item source. To keep the first example simple, we will ignore the actual item loading for now and regard only the component's state change that is involved.

An executable JUnit test is a public, nonstatic method that gets annotated with `@Test` and takes no parameters. Summarizing all this information, the next step could be a method stub that names a functionality of our component we want to test. In our case, this functionality could be the ability to set the fetch-count to a certain amount:

```
public class TimelineTest {
  @Test
  public void setFetchCount() {
  }
}
```

Downloading the example code

You can download the example code files for all Packt books you have purchased from your account at `http://www.packtpub.com`. If you purchased this book elsewhere, you can visit `http://www.packtpub.com/support` and register to have the files e-mailed directly to you.

Additionally, the author has hosted the code sources for this book on his GitHub repository at `https://github.com/fappel/Testing-with-JUnit`. So, you can download it from this URL and work with the code.

This is still not much, but it is actually sufficient to run the test for the first time. JUnit test executions can be launched from the command line or a particular UI. But for the scope of this book, let's assume we have IDE integration available. Within Eclipse, the result would look like the next image.

The green progress bar signals that the test run did not recognize any problems, which is not a big surprise as we have not verified anything yet. But remember that we have already done some useful considerations that help us to populate our first test easily:

- We intend to write the `Timeline` component. To test it, we can create a local variable that takes a new instance of this component.

- As the first test should verify the state-changing effect of setting the item-count attribute, it seems natural to introduce appropriate setters and getters to do so:

```
@Test
public void setFetchCount() {
  Timeline timeline = new Timeline();

  timeline.setFetchCount( 5 );
  int actual = timeline.getFetchCount();
}
```

It looks reasonable so far, but how can we assure that a test run is denoted as a failure if the actual value returned by getFetchCount does not match the input used with setFetchCount? For this purpose, JUnit offers the org.junit.Assert class, which provides a set of static methods to help developers to write so-called self-checking tests.

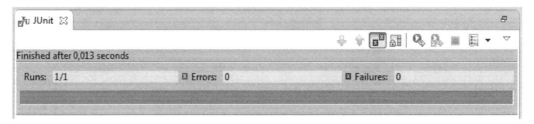

The green bar after a successful launch

The methods prefixed with assert are meant to check a certain condition, throwing an java.lang.AssertionError on a negative evaluation. Such errors are picked up by the tool's runtime and mark the test as failed in the resulting report. To assert that two values or objects are equal, we can use Assert.assertEquals. As it is very common to use static imports for assertion method calls, the getFetchCount test can be completed like this:

```
@Test
public void setFetchCount() {
  Timeline timeline = new Timeline();
  int expected = 5;

  timeline.setFetchCount( expected );
  int actual = timeline.getFetchCount();

  assertEquals( expected, actual );
}
```

The built-in mechanism of JUnit, which is often considered somewhat dated, isn't the only possibility to express test verifications. But to avoid information flooding, we will stick to it for now and postpone a thorough discussion of the pros and cons of alternatives to *Chapter 7, Improving Readability with Custom Assertions*.

Looking at our first test, you can recognize that it specifies a behavior of the SUT, which does not even exist yet. And by the way, this also means that the test class does not compile anymore. So, the next step is to create a skeleton of our component to solve this problem:

```
public class Timeline {

  public void setFetchCount( int fetchCount ) {
  }

  public int getFetchCount() {
    return 0;
  }
}
```

Well, the excitement gets nearly unbearable. What will happen if we run our test against the newly created component?

Evaluating test results

Now the test run leads to a failure with a red progress bar due to the insufficient implementation of the timeline component, as shown in the next image. The execution report shows how many tests were run in total, how many of those terminated with errors, and how many failed due to unmet assertions.

A stack trace for each error/failure helps to identify and understand the problem's cause. AssertionError raised by a verification call of a test provides an explaining message, which is shown in the first line of the trace. In our example, this message tells us that the expected value did not meet the actual value returned by getFetchCount.

A test terminated by an `Exception` indicates an arbitrary programming mistake beyond the test's assertion statements. A simple example of this can be access to an uninitialized variable, which subsequently terminates test execution with `NullPointerException`. JUnit follows the all or nothing principle. This means that if an execution involves more then one test, which is usually the case, a single problem marks the whole suite as failed.

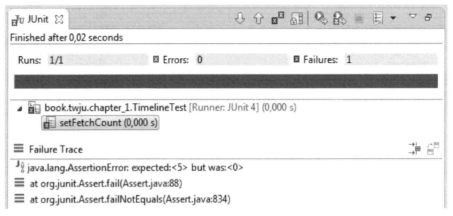

The red bar after test failure

The UI reflects this by painting the progress bar red. You would now wonder whether we shouldn't have completed our component's functionality first. The implementation seems easy enough, and at least, we wouldn't have ended up with the red bar. But the next section explains why starting with a failing test is crucial for a clean test-first approach.

Writing tests first

Writing tests before the production code even exists might look strange to a newbie, but there are actually good reasons to do so. First of all, writing tests after the fact (meaning first code, then test) is no fun at all. Well, that sounds like a hell of a reason because, if *you gotta do what you gotta do*, *[FUTU99]*, what's the difference whether you do it first or last?

The difference is in the motivation to do it right! Once you are done with the fun part, it is all too human to get rid of the annoying duties as fast and as sloppily as one can get through. You are probably reading this because you are interested in improving things. So, ask yourself how effective tests will be if they are written just for justification or to silence the conscience.

Even if you are disciplined and motivated to do your after the fact tests right, there will be more holes in the test coverage compared to the test-first approach. This is because the class under test was not designed for testing. Most of the time, it will take costly steps to decompose a component written from scratch into separate concerns that can be tested easily. And if these steps are considered too expensive, testing will be omitted. But isn't it a bad thing to change a design for testing purposes?

> *"Separation of Concerns' is probably the single most important concept in software design and implementation."*

> – *[HUTH03]*

The point is that writing your tests first supports proper separation implicitly. Every time your test setup feels overly complicated, you are about to put too much functionality in your component. In this case, you should reconsider your class-level design and split it up into smaller pieces. Following this practice consequently leads to a healthy design on the class level out of the box.

Although this book is not about how to write tests first or **test-driven development** (**TDD**) as it is usually called, it follows this principle while developing the example application. But as the focus will be on getting unit tests right and not on the implementation aspects of the components, here come a few words about the work paradigm of TDD for better understanding.

The procedure is simple. Once you have picked your first work unit, write a test, make it run, and last, make it right, *[BECK03]*. After you're done, start it all over again with the next piece of functionality. This is exactly what we have done until now with our first test. We've decided about a small feature to implement. So, we wrote a test that specifies the intended behavior and invented a kind of programming interface that would match the use case.

When we feel confident with the outcome, it is about time to fix the compile errors and create a basic implementation stub to be able to execute the test. This way, the test is the first client of the freshly created component, and we will have the earliest possible feedback on how using it in programs will look. However, it is important that the first test run fails to ensure that the verification conditions were not met by accident.

The make it run step is about fixing the failing test as quickly as possible. This goal outweighs everything else now. We are even allowed to commit programming sins we usually try to avoid. If this feels a bit outlandish, think of it like this: if you want to write clean code that works (*Ron Jeffries, [BECK03]*) ensure that it works first and then take your time and clean it up second. This has the advantage that you know the specification can be met without wasting time in writing pretty code that will never work.

Last but not least, make it right. Once your component behaves as specified, ascertain that your production and test code follow the best programming standards you can think of. While overhauling your code, repeatedly executing the tests ensures that the behavior is kept intact. Changing code without changing its behavior is called **refactoring**.

In the overall image, we started with a failing test and a red bar, fixed the test, made the bar green again, and, finally, cleaned up the implementation during a last *refactor* step. As this pattern gets repeated over and over again in TDD, it is known as the red/green/refactor mantra.

So, always remember folks: keep the bar green to keep the code clean.

Summary

In this chapter, you learned why unit tests are such a valuable asset for Java developers. We've seen that well-written tests go beyond pure regression avoidance and experienced how they improve your code quality, increase your overall development pace, enhance your component specifications, and, last but not least, convey confidence and courage to your team members.

We've addressed the tool set that accompanies JUnit and prepared our workspace to be able to take active part in the following chapters. After the introduction of the ongoing example, which will serve us as the motivation and source for code snippets for the various subjects, we elaborated a definition of what unit testing is all about. Then, the time came to learn the very basics of writing and executing our first self-checking test. We concluded with an overview of the essentials of TDD, which prepared you for the following topics when you come to know more advanced unit testing techniques.

By continuously evolving our example, the next chapter will reveal the common structure of well-written unit tests. You'll learn some heuristics to pick the next behavior to implement and, finally, gain some insights into unit test naming conventions.

2
Writing Well-structured Tests

In this chapter, we're going to learn how to write unit tests with a clean and consistent structure by means of the four-phase pattern, and outline why it is important to do so. We'll be explaining the purpose of a fixture, and how to get a clear definition of the relation between a component's behavior and its verification. Furthermore, we're going to gain insight on what to test, where to start, how to continue, and how to know when we are done. We'll be concluding with a discussion on the pros and cons of various testing naming conventions. In a nutshell, we will be going through the following topics:

- The four phases of a unit test
- Choosing the next functionality to test
- Getting the test names right

The four phases of a unit test

Well-written unit tests follow a clean and consistent structure based on four exactly defined phases. In this section, we will learn about the purpose of each of those and delve into some subtleties of fixture setup and result verification.

Using a common test structure

"A tidy house, a tidy mind."

– Old adage

The attentive reader may have wondered why our first test `setFetchCount` was segmented by the use of empty lines. To answer this question, let's have an in-depth look at each of these segments with the first listing of this section, showing the common structure of a unit test. There are minor refactorings and additional comments compared to the version in the last chapter to emphasize more on the separation.

Note how the constant `NEW_FETCH_COUNT` replaces the literal value assigned previously to a local input variable. Literal numbers often tell little or nothing about their purpose because they emerge from nowhere like a kind of miracle. Hence, they are often denoted as **magic numbers**.

Constants can improve the awareness of the situation, since a meaningful name is able to unveil, at least to some extent, what the number is all about. Besides, they allow defining values in a way that ensures that they differ from the component defaults. This guarantees that the test action has an effect, but hides the uninteresting details away from the test method itself.

```java
private final static int NEW_FETCH_COUNT
  = Timeline.DEFAULT_FETCH_COUNT + 1;

@Test
public void setFetchCount() {
  // (1) setup (arrange, build)
  Timeline timeline = new Timeline();

  // (2) exercise (act, operate)
  timeline.setFetchCount( NEW_FETCH_COUNT );

  // (3) verify (assert, check)
  assertEquals( NEW_FETCH_COUNT, timeline.getFetchCount() );
}
```

Looking at the preceding example, the common structure of a unit test is as follows:

(1) The first section creates an instance of the object to be tested. This is referred to as **system under test (SUT)**, *[MESZ07]*. In general, this section establishes the SUT's related state *prior* to any test activities. Because this state constitutes well-defined test input and preconditions, it is also called the **fixture** of a test.

(2) After the fixture has been initialized, it is time to invoke that functionality of the SUT whose behavior the test intends to check. Often, this is just a single method, and the outcome gets stored in local variables. In our test, we are interested in the new value of fetch-count, and for compactness, its retrieval is in-lined.

(3) The last section verifies that the outcome actually matches the specified behavior. In our case, we expect the actual fetch-count to be equal to the value of the `NEW_FETCH_COUNT` constant.

Structuring a test like this is very common and has been described by various authors. It has been labelled as an arrange, act, assert, *[BECK03]* or build, operate, check, *[MART09]* pattern. But I'd like to be thorough for once, and stick to the Meszaros' (*[MESZ07]*) terminology of the *four* phases called setup (1), exercise (2), verify (3), and teardown (4), in this book. So let's conclude with an explanation of the fourth phase, which isn't a part of the previous listing.

(4) A test should leave its environment in the same condition as it was in before the execution of the test. Because of this, it is supposed to clean up any persistent state. The latter implies conditions created during setup or exercise that survive the end of a test. And this may influence a test's successor unfavorably. Think, for example, of a system property set to evoke a specific behavior of a component. Teardown should take care of a proper reset at the end of a test. This is important as most subsequent tests probably don't expect the property to be set and might fail due to this unexpected side effect.

Plain unit tests rarely have to deal with the persistent state, so teardown is, as in our example, often omitted. And since it is completely irrelevant from the specification point of view, we'd like to keep it out of the test method anyway. We'll see soon how this can be achieved with JUnit.

Given the introduction of the common unit test structure, you might ask yourself, "What's the point, why is this so important?".

> *"The ratio of time spent reading (code) versus writing is well over 10 to 1…"*
>
> – *Robert C. Martin, Clean Code, [MART09]*

A four-phases-pattern test expresses the objective of a test clearly. Setup always defines the test's precondition, exercise actually invokes the functionality under test, and verify checks the expected outcome that constitutes a component's behavior. Last, but not least, teardown is all about housekeeping, as Meszaros (*[MESZ07]*) puts it.

The common structure and clean separation increases readability tremendously. As you're aware of the purpose of each section, you *know* where to look if you need to understand, for example, the test-specific precondition. As a consequence, this approach implies that one test verifies only a particular behavior for a given input state at a time. This is why unit tests normally do without conditional blocks or the like (single-condition test, *[MESZ07]*).

Especially for rookies, it is tempting to avoid the allegedly tedious fixture setup and check as much as possible within a single method. But this usually leads to obfuscation by nature. Compared to the structure described here, crabbed tests make it very hard to grasp the writer's intention. Changes will get more difficult, and maintainability or enhancement cycles will take longer. So remember:

> "*The road to hell is paved with good intentions.*"

> *– Old proverb*

When written badly, tests can make things even worse than they were before. Resist the urge and structure your test properly, even if it takes some time to carve out a test's precondition. But to ease your first steps on the latter, we'll have a closer look at some fixture setup practices now.

Setting up the fixture

As mentioned earlier, a test's fixture setup includes all the activities necessary to prepare a well-defined input state on which a component's functionality is invoked. This may affect things like component creation, setting of particular values, registering of test doubles, and so on.

In our very simple example, all it needs is the creation of a new timeline instance. But most of the time, a test case consists of more than a single test. We might consider it a good idea to check that the initial value of our timeline fetch-count is greater than zero. Thus, we add a test `initialState` to verify exactly this behavior, as shown in the next listing:

```
public class TimelineTest {

  private final static int NEW_FETCH_COUNT
    = new Timeline().getFetchCount() + 1;

  @Test
  public void setFetchCount() {
    Timeline timeline = new Timeline();
```

```
    timeline.setFetchCount( NEW_FETCH_COUNT );

    assertEquals( NEW_FETCH_COUNT, timeline.getFetchCount() );
  }

  @Test
  public void initialState() {
    Timeline timeline = new Timeline();

    assertTrue( timeline.getFetchCount() > 0 );
  }
}
```

> Mind how reflecting about the initial component state has influenced our
> NEW_FETCH_COUNT constant definition.
>
> ```
>     .. NEW_FETCH_COUNT = new Timeline().getFetchCount() + 1;
> ```
>
> As we can expect the default value to be a positive integer, we derive the
> constant from the initial fetch-count setting. This way, we make the test
> less dependent on the component internals. It is quite natural that a test
> case matures while adding more and more specifications. So don't be
> too keen on getting everything perfect, right from the start. Usually, *good*
> means it's a little step that's *good enough* to begin with.

As you can see, initialState leaves out the exercise phase. This is hardly
surprising, as it checks whether the initial component state matches certain criteria.
You may look at it as verifying the outcome of the component's creation, which melts
the phases setup and the exercise into a single statement.

The two timeline tests have their fixture definition within their body. This situation
is called **in-line setup**, *[MESZ07]*. But since the definition is the same for both, it is
a clear case of redundancy, which we usually like to avoid. Hence, we could choose
delegate setup, *[MESZ07]*, to move the common code into a method called by each
test, as shown in the following snippet:

```
@Test
public void setFetchCount() {
  Timeline timeline = createTimeline();

  timeline.setFetchCount( NEW_FETCH_COUNT );

  assertEquals( NEW_FETCH_COUNT, timeline.getFetchCount() );
```

```
    }

    @Test
    public void initialState() {
      Timeline timeline = createTimeline();

      assertTrue( timeline.getFetchCount() > 0 );
    }

    private static Timeline createTimeline() {
      return new Timeline();
    }
```

The method createTimeline is actually a special delegation variant called **create method**, *[MESZ07]*, because its only purpose is to create a new instance of the SUT. Of course, it is dubious whether the delegation improves readability in our very trivial case. But keep in mind that component creation often involves initialization of values or reference components needed as constructor arguments. However, since these arguments might be unimportant and thus disturbing for the understanding of a given test, delegation can be useful even if no redundancy is involved.

At any rate, delegate setup bridges to an interesting feature of JUnit: the possibility to execute a common test setup implicitly. Implicit setup, *[MESZ07]*, can be achieved with the annotation @Before applied to a public, nonstatic method that has no return value and arguments. But this feature comes at a price. If we want to eliminate the redundant createTimeline calls within the tests, we have to introduce a field that takes an instance of Timeline (see the following listing):

```
    public class TimelineTest {

      private final static int NEW_FETCH_COUNT
        = new Timeline(). getFetchCount() + 1;

      private Timeline timeline;

      @Before
      public void setUp() {
        timeline = new Timeline();
      }

      @Test
      public void setFetchCount() {
        timeline.setFetchCount( NEW_FETCH_COUNT );

        assertEquals( NEW_FETCH_COUNT, timeline.getFetchCount() );
      }
```

```
@Test
public void initialState() {
  assertTrue( timeline.getFetchCount() > 0 );
}
}
```

It's evident that implicit setup can remove a lot of code duplication, but it also introduces a kind of magic from the test's point of view. This makes it harder to read. So the clear answer to the question *which kind of setup type should one use* is: it depends.

When we painstakingly pay attention to keep components and test cases small, the trade-off seems acceptable. Then, implicit setup can be used to define the fixture common for all tests. Small in-line and delegate setup statements may supplement the specific preconditions on per-test basis. But as beginners often tend to let classes grow too large, it might be better to stick with the in-line and delegate setup first.

Before actually executing a test, the JUnit runtime creates a new instance of the test class. This means that the simple fixture in our example could omit the setUp method completely. Assignment of the timeline field with a fresh fixture could be done implicitly like this:

```
private final Timeline timeline = new Timeline();
```

While some people use this a lot, other people argue that the @Before annotated method makes the intention more explicit, which is why we'll stick to the annotated version throughout this book.

Now that we know how to set up a fixture properly, one might wonder how to get rid of it neatly in case it is persistent?

What goes up must come down

Imagine for a moment that a Timeline instance would produce a persistent state and needs to be disposed of. This means that we have to add a teardown phase to our tests. Based on the current TimelineTest class, this is an easy thing to do. JUnit supports **implicit teardown** in conjunction with the @After annotation. We would only have to add the following implicit teardown method:

```
@After
public void tearDown() {
  timeline.dispose();
}
```

As explained earlier, teardown is all about housekeeping and adds no information to a particular test. Because of this, it is convenient to perform it implicitly. Alternatively, one would have to handle this with a **try-finally** construct around the exercise and verify statements to ensure that the clean-up gets done even if a test fails. Unfortunately, the latter construct decreases readability notably since it creates an overhead of inner blocks (see the following snippet).

```java
@Test
public void setFetchCount() {
  Timeline timeline = new Timeline();

  try {
    timeline.setFetchCount( NEW_FETCH_COUNT );

    assertEquals( NEW_FETCH_COUNT, timeline.getFetchCount() );
  } finally {
    timeline.dispose();
  }
}
```

Verification

As previously mentioned, a unit test verifies only one behavior at a time. We define behavior as the outcome of a component's functionality applied under given circumstances. The following diagram shows how this definition maps to the phases of a unit test and, in particular, how the verify phase checks the behavior's outcome:

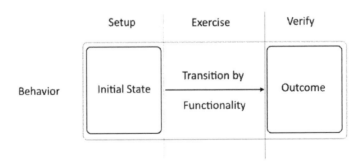

Relation of behavior and unit test phases

For example, under the condition that our timeline component already contains some items in a sorted order (*initial state*), the functionality *adding an item* behaves correctly with respect to our specification (*transition*), if afterwards the component contains all old items, plus the new ones, in a sorted order (*outcome*).

It is important to understand that behavior shows its effects not only in one or more state changes, but also in interactions like notifications of other components. Overall, there might be various things to check to ensure correctness. There is a school of thought propagating a one-assert-per-test policy, but in the light of the preceding explanations, it appears more obvious to use a single-concept-per-test idea, *[MART09]*. If you put concept on a level with behavior, it is evident that verification is not limited to just one assertion as it, incidentally, happens to be in our simple listings.

Note that a detailed discussion on verification techniques will be provided in *Chapter 7, Improving Readability with Custom Assertions*. For now, we'll leave it at that and go on writing more tests.

Choosing the next functionality to test

Now that you know how to structure a test properly, you still might feel a bit insecure about what to test, where to start, how to continue, and how to know when you are done. What follows will be a few heuristics to help you in mastering these hurdles.

Start with the happy path

Meszaros defines the happy path as *the normal path of execution through a use case or the software that implements it; also known as the sunny day scenario. Nothing goes wrong, nothing out of the ordinary happens, and we swiftly and directly achieve the user's or caller's goal, [MESZ07]*. Regarding the addition of an item to our timeline functionality, the happy path is made up of an item that gets sorted into a list of existing items, and hence, gets depicted at the correct chronological position.

But what makes it so important to start with it? Because it delivers the highest business value, and gets us closer to the component's expected capabilities. Once we are done with the normal path of execution, we know that a specification can be met. Starting with boundary conditions, we might waste time if we recognize later on that the prime scenario does not work out well. Furthermore, it seems that the code for boundary conditions often hinders a straightforward sunny day implementation when done last, whereas corner case code can be integrated easily into a main scenario most of the time.

Since a component might have several functionalities to offer, it is quite possible to have more than one happy path per test case. Similar to the aforementioned reasoning, it is plausible in such situations to start with the implementation that offers the highest business value. But sometimes, it may also be suitable to begin with a low hanging fruit, *[KACZ13]*, that is, a very simple functionality.

This is particularly useful if you are stuck and not yet completely sure about where to go. Commencing like this, you probably gain some insights on the more complex tasks ahead. You may have noticed by now that this is exactly the approach we took with our example listings. So hopefully, you've obtained a lot of knowledge by now! But how do we continue after we're done with the main course of action?

Conclude with corner cases

> *"There are two hard things in computer science: cache invalidation, naming things, and off-by-one errors."*
>
> *– [FOWL2H]*

While the happy path scenario usually represents the highest business value, you're not done once your component under test meets the main requirements. On the contrary, the nastiest problems can occur with respect to boundary conditions and might be spotted rather late. This is because they often appear on less frequently used but important paths of execution.

It is necessary to recognize these corner cases and cover them with tests. To make sure that our timeline's paging mechanism gets shielded from unreasonable fetch-count settings, one might limit the allowed attribute values to an appropriate range. Additional tests ensure that input values exceeding the boundaries are not accepted.

```java
@Test
public void setFetchCountExceedsLowerBound() {
  int originalFetchCount = timeline.getFetchCount();

  timeline.setFetchCount( Timeline.FETCH_COUNT_LOWER_BOUND - 1 );

  assertEquals( originalFetchCount, timeline.getFetchCount() );
}

@Test
public void setFetchCountExceedsUpperBound() {
  int originalFetchCount = timeline.getFetchCount();
```

```
timeline.setFetchCount( Timeline.FETCH_COUNT_UPPER_BOUND + 1 );

assertEquals( originalFetchCount, timeline.getFetchCount() );
}
```

We have chosen to provide the values that define our range boundaries as constants. Now we can use them to find the first value that exceeds an affected boundary. This way, changing the range value definitions later on does not affect our test code. At the end, we specify that out-of-bounds values should be ignored, which is expressed by the `assertEquals` verifications.

> The latter is probably not the brightest design decision as it may obscure misbehaving client calls. In general, it is better to quit invalid input values with `IllegalArgumentException`. This approach would follow the fail fast pattern, *[SHOR04]*, with the intention to reveal the programming mistakes at the earliest possible point in time.
>
> But nobody is immune from making bad calls, and so it might be helpful to show how sound test cases can adapt easily to low level specifications evolving over time. We'll come back to this topic in *Chapter 4, Testing Exceptional Flow*.

But how can we make sure that we have tested all the necessary corner cases? *Hunt and Thomas, [HUTH03]*, have introduced the acronym **CORRECT** to provide a checklist that one can go through to localize potential hotspots. The acronym CORRECT stands for:

- **Conformance**: Does a value conform to an expected format?
- **Ordering**: Is a set of values ordered appropriately?
- **Range**: Is a value within a minimum and maximum definition?
- **Reference**: Is there a reference to anything external that isn't controlled by your component (notifications)?
- **Existence**: Does the value exist (for example not null, non-zero, present in a set, and so on)?
- **Cardinality**: Are there exactly enough values?
- **Time (absolute and relative)**: Is everything happening in order? At the right time? In time?

While this is a fine starting point, you'll pretty soon develop a good sense of what cases have to be covered. And if you happen to miss something? Well, this will happen! Then proceed as mentioned in *Chapter 1, Getting Started*. Once the problem occurs, add a new test that reproduces the malfunction with a failing verification. Change your code to get all your tests green. After that, you can go on with your life as the issue will be solved sustainably.

After the war

> "*Test Driven Development is a very useful, but certainly not sufficient, tool to help you get good tests.*"

> – *Martin Fowler, [FOWL12]*

So in rare cases, it may happen that we think we are done with all the boundary conditions, but have still overlooked something due to a conceptual error or the like. At this development stage, it can be valuable to use a code coverage tool to find out if we have missed any paths of execution.

Consider, for example, that we have inadvertently deleted the `@Test` annotation of the `setFetchCountExceedsUpperBound` test. Running our tests while recording coverage would reveal that the path responsible to meet the respective requirement does not get executed. The image Incomplete Test Coverage shows how the statement matching the start point of the exceeds-upper-bound-condition-branch is marked with a yellow background.

```java
public class Timeline {

  public static final int FETCH_COUNT_LOWER_BOUND = 1;
  public static final int FETCH_COUNT_UPPER_BOUND = 20;

  private static final int DEFAULT_FETCH_COUNT = 10;

  private int fetchCount;

  public Timeline() {
    fetchCount = DEFAULT_FETCH_COUNT;
  }

  public void setFetchCount( int fetchCount ) {
    if(    fetchCount >= FETCH_COUNT_LOWER_BOUND
        && fetchCount <= FETCH_COUNT_UPPER_BOUND )
    {
      this.fetchCount = fetchCount;
    }
  }

  public int getFetchCount() {
    return fetchCount;
  }
}
```

Incomplete test coverage

This is problematic as we now have a gap in our safety net. One could easily break the component's behavior by changing the marked line without being noticed. Of course, the example is based on a simple mistake, which can be fixed quickly. But according to Brian Marick, such gaps may be an indication of a more fundamental problem in your test case called **faults of omission**, *[MARI]* (these are explained in detail in *Chapter 8, Running Tests Automatically within a CI Build*). So it might be advisable to reconsider the affected test cases completely.

Code coverage can detect holes and, therefore, potential trouble with respect to our component's correctness. But note that the reverse conclusion is not valid. Completeness of coverage doesn't ensure that we have tested every potential behavior. Adding a single statement to a covered path of execution might alter the outcome of a test's exercise phase and still pass all of its existing verifications.

Having said this, please note that full coverage is not always achievable or would be unreasonably expensive to achieve. So be careful not to overdo things. To quote Martin Fowler again:

> *"I would be suspicious of anything like 100% – it would smell of someone writing tests to make the coverage numbers happy, but not thinking about what they are doing."*

> *– [FOWL12]*

So now that we've learned a lot about the nature of a well structured test and how to evolve test cases efficiently, let's turn towards the *real* difficult task: how to name our tests concisely.

Getting the test names right

Finding good names is one of the challenges of crafting software. You need to find them all the time and for everything: classes, methods, variables, just to name a few. Because of that, the last section of this chapter explains the particularities of naming tests and balances the pros and cons of common approaches and conventions.

Test prefix

What makes a name a good name? To quote Uncle Bob:

> *"Three things: Readability, readability, and readability!"*

He defines this later on as clarity, simplicity, and density of expression, *[MART09]*. Though this sounds reasonable, it leaves us with the question of how to achieve these qualities when naming our tests.

Before the arrival of annotations in the Java language, it was necessary to distinguish tests from ordinary methods to be able to process them by the JUnit runtime. This is because the latter has to pick up each test separately, run it, and report the results. The technical solution was to prefix the name of public, nonstatic methods that do without return values and arguments with *test* to denote them as executable. As a result, a test case was a compound of various methods called `testFoo`, `testBar`, and so on.

Unfortunately, this prefix adds little to nothing to the intention revealing purpose of a test name, but rather increases the clutter or even worse it sometimes makes it more difficult to find a name that can be read fluently. That's why, the designers of JUnit decided, once annotations were around, to mark JUnit executables with `@Test`. Since then, the prefix approach is obsolete, and the name can be chosen at will. But as is often the case, bad habits die hard, and so this convention is still used a lot.

Notwithstanding the above, developer's strived early on for naming conventions that focused on the behavior related nature of unit tests and at which we'll have a look now.

Behavior-expressing patterns

One of the trend-setting work in behavior related naming conventions was Roy Osherove's post on *Naming Standards for Unit Tests, [OSHE05]*. He postulated that a test name *should express a specific requirement* and *should include the expected input or state and the expected result for that input or state*.

 Note that this is fairly close to our behavior definition and the unit test structure given previously.

The resulting pattern that he proposed separates the different responsibilities with underscores, and looks like this:

```
[UnitOfWork_StateUnderTest_ExpectedBehavior]
```

So if we look again at the addition of an item to our timeline example, we deduce that the unit of work is adding an item. The state under test is reflected by the timeline's list of already added items (in sorted order, which probably means at least two). Last but not least, the expected behavior (which we refer to more precisely as outcome) results in the list of correctly sorted items that now also contains the newly added one.

Trying to translate these considerations into a meaningful name according to Osherove's standards, we might end up somewhat like this:

```
addItem_hasListOfSortedItems_listContainsAdditionalItemAndIsSorted
```

You can see that the name is actually a compound of three names, each of which uses camel case notation to express its purpose in a fluently readable fashion. The idea is that anyone should get a fairly good understanding of the component's behavior simply by browsing through the method names of a component's test case.

However, underscores are somewhat frowned upon in Java and some people claim that unit test names ought to focus on the *scenario* (probably the outcome of our way of looking at things). A popular approach in this area starts with the `should` prefix to express the test's intention. In Osherove's terms, an abstraction of this pattern might be written as follows:

```
[shouldExpectedBehaviorWhenUnitOfWorkOnStateUnderTest]
```

Once again, we can try to translate our example into a name, but this time starting with the `should` prefix followed by the expected behavior.

```
shouldContainAdditionalItemAndIsSortedWhenAddItemOnListOfSortedItems
```

Well, maybe our examples are overdoing things a bit, but unfortunately, names following these patterns tend to lack clarity and simplicity of expression. In particular, the last name makes it difficult for our in-brain-parser to distinguish the behavior defining segments at one glance. While the underscores make the differentiation easier, in case of multiple preconditions and outcomes, one still has to dig deep to grasp what a test is all about.

The reason for this is that we are looking for a meaningful name, not a comprehensive specification. A one liner is simply not able to cope with the information density of a complex behavior. The latter brought Dan North to the idea of **behavior-driven development** (BDD), where test names should be sentences, *[NORT06]*. He even created an alternative testing framework, *[JBEHAV]*. This allows writing of tests in a textual Given-When-Then structure, and maps each line to an annotated Java test step method. The following listing gives an idea of a textural description based on our example:

```
Given the timeline contains two sorted items

When a new item gets added to the timeline

Then the timeline contains all old items
 And the timeline contains the newly added one
 And the timeline is sorted correctly
```

Fowler clarifies that the different step types can be mapped to our four-phase test structure like this: given = > setup, when => exercise, and then => verify (in case you wonder, BDD has no teardown equivalent), *[FOWL13]*. Some developers even emphasize this by adding comments before each phase using the BDD step identifiers, as shown in the next variant of `setFetchCountExceedsLowerBound` with BDD step identifiers:

```
@Test
public void setFetchCountExceedsLowerBound() {
  // given
  int originalFetchCount = timeline.getFetchCount();

  // when
  timeline.setFetchCount( Timeline.FETCH_COUNT_LOWER_BOUND - 1 );

  // then
  assertEquals( originalFetchCount, timeline.getFetchCount() );
}
```

But how can these considerations help us to improve our test names?

Reducing names to the essentials

The point of the BDD turnaround was to remind us that we already have the complete behavior specification in our unit test. We don't need to force this information redundantly into the test's name! The more information we put into it, the harder it is to read and the likelier it is that it gets outdated, as code documentation often does.

For example, when changing an expected outcome from *ignoring a certain input value* to *throwing an exception on that value*, it can easily happen that the developer forgets to update the test's name accordingly. This is symptomatic to all tasks requiring great diligence. There is no compile-time check for those kinds of mistakes and the test case would be misleading, if written in accordance with the conventions introduced previously. But we can avoid this kind of trouble simply by skipping the outcome section entirely.

This is possible as a behavior is unambiguously identifiable by its functionality and the appropriate preconditions. Test cases following that convention simply list the various use case scenarios of the component under test. But as a consequence, one has to step into a method to get an understanding of the expected outcome.

Another simplification is related to the fixture state. In general, test cases share some common setup state, which seldom represents the base for the happy path tests. Corner cases may vary this common state a bit to match their preconditions. Kent Beck notes, for example, that:

> *"If you can't easily find a common place for common setup code, then there are too many objects too tightly intertwined."*

> *– [BECK03]*

So you should probably be able to find a name that spares the mentioning of these common preconditions.

This means that we can ignore the sorted list of initial items in our example when it comes down to naming the tests. Once again using Osherove's terms and starting with the functionality, the pattern is basically shortened to the following:

```
[UnitOfWork_StateUnderTest]
```

With this in mind, the next listing of test method names shows what our example test case could look like using this strategy. Note that the underscore was replaced with a more fluently readable version using words like to, with, or if to get a better binding between the segments:

```
TimelineTest:

addItem
addItemToEmptyList
addItemWithMissingDate
addItemIfThresholdHasBeenReached
addItemWithNull
...
setFetchCount
setFetchCountExceedsLowerBound
setFetchCountExceedsUpperBound
...
```

But where does this leave us now? As the saying goes, the bigger the choice, the harder it is to choose. While brevity is the soul of the wit, there are supporters for any of the described conventions. Rather it is more likely possible to reduce global warming than finding a common denominator on this topic. But no matter how you choose, make sure that at least all your team members follow the same standard. This keeps your test cases consistent and ensures that the poor wretch working on legacy code doesn't run into apoplexy while continuously adjusting to different naming styles.

Summary

In this chapter, we've learned about the structure of a well-written unit test. We've got to know how to use the four phases, that is setup, exercise, verify, and teardown, to map a single test to a certain component behavior. We've addressed the different techniques to set up a test fixture efficiently and illustrated the relation of a behavior to its verification.

Once we were familiar with *how* to write a test, we've been concerned with *what* to test. We've understood why we should always start testing with happy-path scenarios and do the corner cases later on. Moreover, we've been introduced to how code coverage can help detect holes in our safety net.

In the last section, we've discussed the pros and cons of the various test naming conventions. We've learned about the difficulties to map behavior verification into a meaningful name, and showed some possibilities to reduce a test name to the essentials.

The next chapter will evolve our example to make use of component dependencies. We'll learn about depended-on components and how they are related to indirect inputs and outputs of the component under test. We'll look at the importance of test isolation, and how it can be achieved by using stand-in doubles to satisfy dependencies.

3
Developing Independently Testable Units

One of the most difficult parts for JUnit beginners confronted with non-trivial real-world situations is to decompose big requirements into small and independently testable units. At the beginning of this chapter, you're going to learn how requirements can be translated into single responsibility components and how they assemble into a collaborating system.

Next you're going to understand the impact of collaboration dependencies on our testing efforts. Once you're aware of the role of collaborators and how a component under test interacts with them, you'll get to know when it is important to replace them with test doubles.

Continuing our timeline example, we'll look at the use cases and application practices of the various double patterns in depth. After that, you'll learn about the advantages and disadvantages of mock frameworks. You'll also see how to work with generated doubles in practice, based on Mockito.

Last but not least, you'll be introduced to a particular type of classes that, in contrast to doubles, do not collaborate with our component under test, but rather reduce redundancy and decouple test cases by extracting reusable test related functionality.

This chapter contains more theoretical superstructure as compared to the rest of the book, so it's worthwhile to read it thoroughly and comprehend the examples and exercises. This is because once you're familiar with the topics and skills imparted here, you will be forearmed even for the sneakier situations of your daily testing work. The topics covered in this chapter are:

- Decomposing requirements
- Understanding isolation
- Working with test doubles
- Increasing efficiency with mock frameworks
- Using test helpers

Decomposing requirements

Real-world requirements describe the highly diverse behavior of a software under development. Grouping functionality into single responsibilities, which have to play together to accomplish the program's objectives, creates dependencies between the components that implement such responsibilities. In the first section, you'll learn why and how these relations can affect our unit testing efforts.

Separating concerns

"Divide and rule."

– Julius Caesar

So far, we've learned a lot about the basics of unit testing. But real-world software doesn't consist of one simple class whose behavior is specified by a single test case. Hence, we have to reflect a bit about the requirements before actually starting development. At this stage, we try to spot and group together functionality that affects common concerns from a high level point of view. This helps us to assess the interplay of responsibilities and to decide where to begin.

Remembering our timeline specification from *Chapter 1, Getting Started*, we could list functionality on the left side of an index card, whiteboard, or the like. After that, we could think about how to group these coherently and note some meaningful names on the right side. This way, we decompose the list of requirements into separate components and the related data types. Each component abstracts a functionality subset needed to fulfill the timeline's overall behavior.

But how do we recognize if functionality is related? A good starting point is to watch out for the usage of common state or resources. The following image shows an excerpt of functionality and components/data types that we could have come up with. See that we've noted, for example, the types `Item` and `ItemProvider`.

The index card timeline

We've done that to represent the ability to load the structured data records from arbitrary sources. It is related to the functionality of fetching items page wise (*fetch items page wise*), or fetching items that are newer than the latest locally buffered one (*fetch new items*). The common denominator is the external resource providing access to those data records. It might be a web service, database, e-mail server, and suchlike. Taken as a whole, we've worked out that the responsibility of loading items will be abstracted by the item-provider components. Their implementations will have to supply several methods with specific semantics, all related to the functionality of item retrieval.

In general, we should respect the *single responsibility principle* that claims a component should have one, and only one, reason to change. Since the principle defines responsibility as *a reason for change*, this implies that each component should only have one of it—thus the name. Classes that assume more than one responsibility have more than one reason to change. Most of the time, this leads to coupling of concerns, and changing one responsibility may compromise the class's ability to accomplish the other, [MART02].

You recognize that we've already identified the more coarsely grained concerns in the scopes of UI and model representation. This might not be perfect, but we can always do more iterations and refine our findings if we don't feel confident enough to move on. However, we avoid extensive upfront planning. This is because we'll shape the subtleties of our class-level design by means of our testing efforts as we've already learned. So where is the catch?

Component dependencies

"With a little help from my friends."

– Beatles

Separating concerns into particular components is reasonable as it allows to encapsulate state and group related functionality together, and abstract access to external resources. But there is a price tag to it. Components must work together to meet the overall requirements, which means there are dependencies between them. And component interdependencies are the normal case, not the exception.

Dependencies have a huge impact on our testing practices. Components that help others to satisfy their responsibility are often denoted as **collaborators**. A component that depends on collaborators relies on their behavior. As a consequence, the outcome of the functionality that we'd like to verify can be tightly coupled to the outcome of a collaborator's functionality. And before we know it, we end up with a collaborator chain that makes fixture setup cumbersome at best.

Component versus data classes

In Java, we've got the class concept to provide the implementation of a certain type. Throughout this book, we follow a convention that divides classes into the categories data and components. Data classes are compounds of value fields, which may be published by so-called accessor methods or direct field access. Either way, they serve plain, state representational intentions.

Components, by contrast, express a certain responsibility and supply a coherent set of functionality. Instead of exposing state, they encapsulate and treat it as an implementation detail. Components often depend on other components to fulfill their purpose, and define a behavior policy expressed in terms of the programming interface. This allows the pluggable exchange of different implementation variants.

Applying this distinction to the example, Item is a simple data type, while ItemProvider establishes a component declaration whose implementations can be plugged into Timeline instances to handle item retrieval.

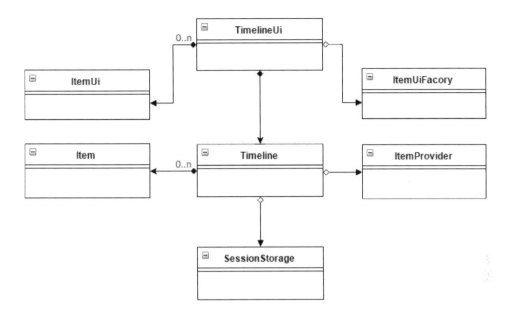

The timeline UML diagram

Suddenly, an image of a provisional architecture arises in our head, and we identify the necessary components and their interactions. But how can we cope with the dependencies that come along in our tests? When we look at the preceding Timeline UML Diagram reflecting our thoughts, we notice, for example, several types providing abstractions to external resources or services.

We intend these abstractions to be types declared by interfaces only. Although we might envision them to look roughly like the following listings, we aim to get a more precise picture once we are writing tests. But as tests won't run with interfaces, it seems that we're stuck.

```
public interface Item {
  long getTimeStamp();
}

public interface ItemProvider {
  List<Item> fetchItems( Item ancestor, int itemCount );
  int getNewCount( Item predecessor );
  List<Item> fetchNew( Item predecessor );
}
```

```
public interface SessionStorage {
  void storeTop( Item top );
  Item readTop();
}
```

The blade we use to cut the Gordian knot (also known as an *impossible knot*, it is an expression for solving an intractable problem by cheating or thinking outside the box) is denoted as **isolation**. With a view to learn how to segregate a component from its collaborators for testing purposes, the next section will start by examining the relationship between both parties more closely.

Understanding isolation

As we've just learned, a component under test usually has to collaborate with other components. But why can this be a problem with respect to unit tests, and what are we going to do about it? This section will explain the necessity of testing functionality in isolation. Afterwards, it introduces the so-called test doubles, which we will use later on to achieve this goal.

Delegating responsibilities to DOCs

Now that we've got a pretty good understanding of the timeline's responsibilities, we want to go ahead with development. As we may consider fetching items from a provider as the most valuable functionality on our way to a minimal viable product, *[MIVIPR]* we decide to continue with page wise fetching.

But we know that a `Timeline` component relies on an `ItemProvider` instance to make this happen. To implement this dependency, we could choose *constructor injection*. Indeed, this binds a certain provider statically to a timeline instance, but it avoids any component reinitialization mechanics that a *setter injection* would demand, *[FOWL04]*.

Expanding the implicit setup of our `TimelineTest`, the following snippet shows what the constructor injection usage would look like. Note the three question marks as we do not know yet where our item provider will emerge from.

```
private ItemProvider itemProvider;
private Timeline timeline;

@Before
public void setUp() {
  itemProvider = ???
  timeline = new Timeline( itemProvider );
}
```

Let's consider for a moment that we would proceed and implement a real-world collaborator that make calls to a remote service to supply us with items. Since the components that we intend to test depend on collaborators, Meszaros denotes the former more generally as **system under test** (**SUT**) and the latter as **depended-on component** (**DOC**), *[MESZ07]*. Using a DOC that encapsulates access to external resources brings along testing related trouble in many respects:

- Depending on the components that we cannot control might impede the decent verification of a test specification. Just think of our real-world web service that could be unavailable at times. This could cause a test failure, although the SUT itself is working properly.

- DOCs might also slow down test execution. To enable unit tests to act as safety net, the complete test-suite of a system under development has to be executed very often. This is only feasible if each test runs incredibly fast. Again think of the web service example.

- Last but not least, the DOC's behavior may change unexpectedly due to the usage of a newer version of the web service API, for example. This shows how depending directly on components we cannot control makes a test fragile.

So what can we do to circumvent these problems?

As we do not want our unit tests to be dependent on the behavior of a DOC, nor do we want them to be slow or fragile, we strive to shield our components as much as possible from all other parts of the software. Flippantly spoken, we make the verification of external resource abstractions from the view point of a unit test to somebody else's problem, *[SOELPR]*.

Often, we set up specific integration tests — and if we want to check the overall system behavior, acceptance tests — that handle such DOCs. The first type verifies that a component meets its specifications, and the second that its incorporation works as expected from an end user's way of looking at things.

In general, the principle introduced here is known as *isolation of the SUT*. It expresses the aspiration to test concerns separately and keep tests independent of each other. Practically, it implies that a component should be designed in such a manner that each DOC can be replaced by a so-called *test double*. This is a lightweight stand-in collaborator used instead of the real DOC, *[MESZ07]*.

With regard to our example, this means we have to provide an implementation of `ItemProvider` that does not make any remote calls to a web service API. This surely keeps our unit test fast. But how can we configure, for example, a stand-in component to supply us with the behavior needed for testing the happy path and corner-case scenarios of our SUT? To answer this question, we need to take a closer look at how SUT and DOCS interact. More precisely, we have to understand the different test related input and output types involved with their communication.

Indirect input and output

So far, our testing efforts confronted us with *direct* inputs and outputs of the SUT only. They are denoted as **direct** because our test code communicates by itself with the SUT. Changing the fetch-count attribute of a `Timeline` instance or reading its current state are examples of a direct input and output respectively. Direct inputs are used to configure an SUT during setup and direct outputs are devoted to verify the outcome of an expected behavior. This relation is shown in the following image:

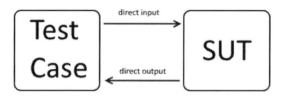

Direct inputs and outputs

But with DOCs involved, the situation gets a bit more complicated. Consider an `ItemProvider` instance supplying items by its `fetchItems` method. Its signature is declared in the interface sketch further up. As we're about to implement a fetching mechanism for our timeline model, we depend on the items provided by our collaborator's fetch functionality. From the SUT's point of view, the items are **indirect input** as they're reachable only via the item provider detour.

Interestingly enough, the items made available as indirect input will serve as direct output once the fetch call of the timeline instance under test has been exercised. This way, we check whether the expected items (indirect input) have been made available in the timeline's data structure (direct output). This path of state transfer can be followed in the following image by the two arrows at the bottom:

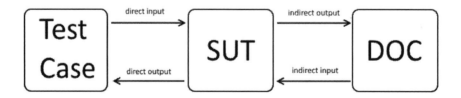

Different types of inputs and outputs

To be able to restore a `Timeline` instance after system restart, we could expect *that each state change due to an item fetch run gets persisted*. This could be achieved by dispatching the current state to the storage each time a call to `fetchItems` or `fetchNew` occurs. Because of this, we've already started to think about a collaborator, `SessionStorage`.

But instead of buffering the complete content, we consider it sufficient for the moment, if the DOC persists the timeline's latest top item which avoids missing out items released after the last session has been halted. On a restart, the timeline fetches its first list of items starting with the buffered one.

If we look at the timeline directly, there is no chance to find out whether saving the most recent item has happened or not. There is no state change of the SUT involved. But we can check if the item has reached the collaborator via its `storeTop` method. This kind of data transfer is called **indirect output**. As saving is a side effect of fetching, this time, the path of state transfer is more difficult to comprehend. The item to save is not provided as direct input to the SUT. Instead, it is derived from the items supplied as indirect input of the item provider component.

Given these explanations, we're now able to see the big picture and understand the advantages, but we should also recognize some pitfalls that one has to keep in mind.

Unit isolation with test doubles

Summarizing what we've learned so far in this chapter, in unit tests, we replace expensive DOCs with cheap test doubles. In doing so, we separate our SUT from the undesirable effects induced by real-world collaborators. And this, in turn, ensures that the functionality under test gets executed in isolation from the functionality we can't control.

Furthermore, we gain authority over indirect inputs and outputs, which allows us to set up a specific fixture state and verify the expected outcome in our tests efficiently. The next section will bring an in-depth explanation of how to apply the various test double design patterns on the basis of our ongoing timeline example.

> *"Where there is light, there must be shadow..."*
>
> – *Haruki Murakami*

But before we move on, it's important to note that there is a trade-off when working with replacements. A problem arises if stand-in components do not mimic the genuine collaborator correctly. This can easily falsify the test results. We mentioned earlier the importance of validating the correctness of expensive collaborators with integration tests. But having a flawed replacement in our unit test opens a gap in our safety net. This is because the test verifies the outcome that would have been different if the stand-in would have behaved correctly.

Because of this, we must place emphasis on meeting the common specification exactly. Figuratively speaking, we don't want to come to a situation where we build perfect cars for crash-test dummies, but fail on real humans. On that account, it seems reasonable to cover the stand-in components with separate test cases in extraordinary complex scenarios. However, these scenarios seldom use the test-first approach, and so we usually go without the extra double tests.

Another difficulty originates from the fact that replacement components often simulate only partial behavior. Just enough to pass a test. But sometimes, there can be more than one way to implement a certain functionality when backed by a collaborator. It is possible, for example, to check that a `Collection` is empty by either using `size` or the convenient method `isEmpty`. So consider that we replace a collection with a stand-in implementation that provides only the size variant, because this is the one used by the component under test.

Although it would be completely reasonable, we were not be able to refactor the code to use the empty check without breaking our test case. The good news is that if we've worked thoroughly, the problem wouldn't go unnoticed. But it is annoying as we run into unnecessary effort to make the refactoring work unnecessary since we have technically used equivalent approaches.

This trivial example shows how inapt double usage couples tests tightly to SUT implementation details. And having such tight coupling in real-world scenarios can hinder maintenance and feature enhancement significantly. Thus, we do not use stand-in components for lightweight collaborators or data structures. The approach described here is meant to be used where access to resources (database, file system, or the like) via software components (database driver, file system API, and so on) should be encapsulated by adapters. Such adapters serve as collaborators for the functionality provided by the components we write on our own.

But before concluding this section, one last advice: Make sure you define your *own* collaborator types, and beware of using third-party library or framework interfaces! This way, you determine a clear boundary between your application and the third-party code. In case a new library version introduces a slightly different behavior, you simply have to adjust your adapter code to make an corresponding integration test pass again. Your actual application code, including the unit tests, will stay unaffected!

In addition, you can switch to another vendor easily by providing an appropriate adapter, which is what the timeline uses to be able to connect to different service providers. But not less important is that you define the collaborator's behavior in your own terms. This helps to avoid train wrecks, *[TRAWRE]*, or the like, in cases where the required functionality is spread over several third-party components. Writing your own adapter will pay off as unit tests can be written more smoothly without undergoing the setup litany of creating a web of test doubles replacing the third-party functionality.

Finally, after all this theoretical elucidations, it is time to see how we use test doubles in practice.

Working with test doubles

Test doubles serve various purposes like indirect input provisioning, recording of indirect output, or immediate verification of interactions. So it can hardly be surprising that there are quite a few different types of double patterns. This section introduces them and gives examples of hand-written implementations, which should be a precious experience for a deep comprehension and the correct application of stand-in components.

Placeholder dummies

To get a component into a state that constitutes a test's precondition, it is sometimes necessary to satisfy dependencies to collaborators which do not actually contribute to the functionality under test. The only right to exist for these DOCs is to fill in argument lists to avoid input verifying exceptions or the like. Because of this, it is superfluous for the stand-in to provide any real functionality. A test double that serves this role is denoted as **dummy**.

Let's assume our enhanced `Timeline` constructor checks whether the injected `ItemProvider` instance is `null` and quits with an appropriate exception if true. As a consequence, we need to initialize any timeline instance with an item provider, even if it is used to calculate our `NEW_FETCH_COUNT` test constant value only. The following listing shows an appropriate implementation:

```
public class ItemProviderDummy implements ItemProvider {

  private static String MESSAGE
    = "Dummy method must never be called.";

  @Override
  public List<Item> fetchItems( Item ancestor, int fetchCount ) {
```

```
      throw new UnsupportedOperationException( MESSAGE );
    }

    @Override
    public int getNewCount( Item predecessor ) {
      throw new UnsupportedOperationException( MESSAGE );
    }

    @Override
    public List<Item> fetchNew( Item predecessor ) {
      throw new UnsupportedOperationException( MESSAGE );
    }
  }
```

 Looking at the code, you'll notice how every method throws an UnsupportedOperationException error. A dummy is meant to be passed around but not to be used. Throwing this exception ensures that we don't break this contract by accident.

Now let's see how the dummy gets applied in our example code:

```
    private final static int NEW_FETCH_COUNT
      = new Timeline( new ItemProviderDummy() ).getFetchCount() + 1;
```

If the list of constructor arguments grows, this might go beyond our personal readability threshold, and we prefer to extract the calculation into a separate method. If used in more than one test case, it might even be justified to introduce a *test helper* providing these calculations. We'll cover such helpers in the last section of this chapter.

Fake it till you make it

Sometimes, we need a collaborator that actually provides an implementation, but takes one or more shortcuts that makes it unusable for production code. We are not interested in the DOC's indirect inputs or outputs, but rather simply want it to be fast or independent from environmental influences. This type of a stand-in component is called a **fake**.

As we do not need a pure fake double for testing purposes in our timeline example, you may think of an in-memory database as a general example. However, as we'll make use of the abstract `Item` data on many occasions, I take this opportunity to introduce an item implementation `FakeItem` that surely isn't capable of productive assignment:

```
public class FakeItem implements Item {


  private final long timeStamp;
  FakeItem( long timeStamp ) {
    this.timeStamp = timeStamp;
  }

  @Override
  public long getTimeStamp() {
    return timeStamp;
  }
}
```

The only thing our immutable fake item provides is the mandatory time-stamp value needed for ordering. This is sufficient for the quick definition of test input data, which is why we could have just as well named it `TestItem`.

Now we'll continue with the test double patterns that make use of indirect inputs and outputs for SUT isolation and test verification.

Providing indirect input with stubs

It's time to remember that we're still on our way to introduce the capability of fetching items page wise by means of an item provider collaborator. From what we've learned, we'd like to have a test double supplying us a list of items as indirect input.

In general, we like to replace a real object with a test-specific object that feeds the desired indirect inputs into the system under test, *[MESZ07]*. A stand-in component following this pattern is called a **stub**, which implies that we need to implement an `ItemProviderStub`, allowing us to configure the items we are expecting as a test outcome.

Fetching items page wise means that we must be able to load a certain amount of subsequent items starting from a given ancestor. Thinking about the item provider's interface, we thus define a method called `fetchItems`. Along with this, an argument specifying the actual amount of items to load would be helpful, and for follow-up fetches, we should know about the oldest item loaded so far. This leads us to the following signature:

```
List<Item> fetchItems( Item ancestor, int fetchCount );
```

To be able to preconfigure an item provider stub with expected result values, we introduce a method `addItems` (see `'location 2'` marker in `ItemProviderStub` in the following listing), which accepts the varargs argument `items`. This way, we can apply more than one item at once. Note that due to the somewhat static form of a book, we anticipate the evolution of the stub a bit. The following listing already supports corner case tests for different fetch conditions:

```java
class ItemProviderStub implements ItemProvider {

  private final Set<Item> items;

  ItemProviderStub() {
    items = new HashSet<>();
  }

  @Override
  // location 1: stub implementation to provide items to fetch
  public List<Item> fetchItems( Item ancestor, int itemCount ) {
    return items
      .stream()
      .sorted( sort() )
      .filter( item -> isApplicable( ancestor, item ) )
      .limit( itemCount )
      .collect( toList() );
  }

  // location 2: method for stub configuration
  void addItems( Item ... itemsToAdd ) {
    items.addAll( asList( itemsToAdd ) );
  }

  private Comparator<? super Item> sort() {
    return ( first, second )
      -> compare( second.getTimeStamp(), first.getTimeStamp() );
  }

  private boolean isApplicable( Item ancestor, Item item ) {
    return    ancestor == null
           || item.getTimeStamp() < ancestor.getTimeStamp();
  }
}
```

The stub simply consists of a set as data structure, containing all the items added for testing purposes. The method fetchItems (see: 'location 1') ensures that the items are sorted chronologically, and only items older than the ancestor (if available) are returned. Last but not least, the returned list is limited to the given item-count.

The considerations about the stub are motivated by the fact that we want to introduce a timeline functionality, which allows us to fetch items page wise from a data source. Having our data source abstraction in place, we can put our plan into practice. We specify a parameter-less method fetchItems to be able to trigger this functionality programmatically.

An appropriate test might configure two fake items as a fixture. During exercise, we expect fetchItems to load these items into the timeline data model, which will represent them afterwards in a chronological order. The outcome state can be retrieved by getItems and will be checked with an assertArrayEquals expression, for example:

```
private static final FakeItem FIRST_ITEM = new FakeItem( 10 );
private static final FakeItem SECOND_ITEM = new FakeItem( 20 );

private ItemProviderStub itemProvider;
private Timeline timeline;

@Before
public void setUp() {
  itemProvider = new ItemProviderStub();
  timeline = new Timeline( itemProvider );
}

@Test
public void fetchItems() {
  itemProvider.addItems( FIRST_ITEM, SECOND_ITEM );

  timeline.fetchItems();
  List<Item> actual = timeline.getItems();

  assertArrayEquals( new Item[] { SECOND_ITEM, FIRST_ITEM },
                     actual.toArray( new Item[ 2 ] ) );
}
```

The preceding listing shows what such a test could look like. But wait a moment! Reconsidering this, it occurs to us that fetching the first items is probably not the happy path, but rather a particular boundary condition. Besides, having fewer items available than the actual fetch-count value seems to be a corner case too. So the normal path of execution should be represented by a subsequent fetch. We could change our test accordingly, as shown in the following snippet:

```
@Test
public void fetchItems() {
    itemProvider.addItems( FIRST_ITEM, SECOND_ITEM, THIRD_ITEM );
    timeline.setFetchCount( 1 );
    timeline.fetchItems();

    timeline.fetchItems();
    List<Item> actual = timeline.getItems();

    assertArrayEquals( new Item[] { THIRD_ITEM, SECOND_ITEM },
                       actual.toArray( new Item[ 2 ] ) );
}
```

The example shows that one could easily get mixed up a bit, identifying the sunny day scenario correctly. Also note how our test actually overshadows the fetch first items behavior. I wouldn't be too worried about running into such subtleties. Skill comes with practice, and refinement of a test case is always possible.

Apropos practice, strictly speaking, the last variant is still a corner case. By now you should be able to locate the restriction, and providing a proper happy path test surely is a good exercise (hint: fetch-count is on the lower bound). After all, our first test versions specify the behavior under particular boundary conditions. But note that we stick for compactness of the item initialization in this chapter with the lower-bound setup.

Now that you're aware of stubbing, think about other corner cases that you have to cover regarding page wise fetching. Write the tests and make them pass by appropriate implementations. Once you feel comfortable with your solution, enhance the timeline's capability further to fetch newer items than those already loaded for example. In the book, we'll continue by introducing test double patterns that make use of indirect output for result verification.

Recording interactions with spies

As explained earlier, we are assuming that fetching new items should persist the most recent item of the data structure after an actual fetch has been processed. This is needed to restore the timeline's state in case the program gets restarted. We have already pondered on a `SessionStore` collaborator that offers the method `storeTop` to acquire this task.

Unfortunately, we are not able to witness the actual storage invocation. Because of this, we decide to use a test double to record the item argument every time the method `storeTop` gets called. This way we can capture the indirect output of our SUT for later verification in our tests. A stand-in component working this way is called a **spy**, *[MESZ07]*. The following listing shows what such an implementation could look like:

```
class SessionStorageSpy implements SessionStorage {

   private final List<Item> log;

   SessionStorageSpy() {
     log = new ArrayList<>();
   }

   @Override
   public void storeTop( Item top ) {
     log.add( top );
   }

   public List<Item> getLog() {
     return log;
   }
}
```

Similar to the item provider, we choose to inject a session storage collaborator as a constructor argument into our timeline instance. Looking at the scenario where we're fetching the first items, we would expect the timeline to store the actual top item once after performing the actual fetch. Our spy captures the indirect storage output in its log data structure. Now a test can use these records for outcome verification. The following snippet shows what this would look like:

```
private SessionStorageSpy sessionStorage;
private ItemProviderStub itemProvider;
private Timeline timeline;

@Before
```

```
public void setUp() {
  itemProvider = new ItemProviderStub();
  sessionStorage = new SessionStorageSpy();
  timeline = new Timeline( itemProvider, sessionStorage );
}

@Test
public void fetchFirstItems() {
  itemProvider.addItems( FIRST_ITEM, SECOND_ITEM );
  timeline.setFetchCount( 1 );

  timeline.fetchItems();
  List<Item> actual = timeline.getItems();

  assertEquals( 1, sessionStorage.getLog().size() );
  assertSame( SECOND_ITEM, sessionStorage.getLog().get( 0 ) );
  [...]
}
```

We can see that the test verifies storeTop has been called once logging the expected item, assuming we find it important to avoid unnecessary storage cycles. As noted previously, restoring the timeline's state more accurately would mean to persist more information about the items loaded. In turn, we'd have to deal with a general data structure as indirect output. We'll see later how to do this with generated doubles.

Besides, as soon as we implement the actual state recovery, we'll have to provide such data as indirect input, and hence need to use a stub again. But this could interfere with our implicit timeline instance setup and the session storage field type. Either we would go back to in-line setup, or write a double that serves both roles. We'll also see later how generated doubles bypass this problem implicitly.

It is obvious that the overall functionality adds quite a few pre - and post - conditions, which is a good opportunity to deepen the skills learned by implementing the additional scenarios as an exercise. But here, we'll continue with a different stand-in component type that also deals with indirect output.

Verifying behavior with mocks

There is another test double pattern that can be used to verify which indirect output gets transferred to storeTop. The most important characteristic of this type is that the verification is performed inside its delegation method. Nonetheless, as we'll see further, it is necessary to ensure that the expected delegation has actually been invoked.

In general, we like to replace an object on which the SUT depends with a test-specific object that verifies it is being used correctly by the SUT, *[MESZ07]*. A stand-in component following this pattern is called a **mock**.

If we start the storage evolution once again with the `storeTop` functionality, a `SessionStorageMock` can be configured with an expected item using a specific setter. In the delegation method, it is immediately checked whether the given item matches the configuration. An additional flag, `storeTopDone`, buffers the information that the method has been called. This allows us to check if the invocation took actually place by using the `verify()` method later on. The next listing shows how this flag also ensures that `storeTop` is not called more than once:

```
class SessionStorageMock implements SessionStorage {

  private boolean storeTopDone;
  private Item expectedTopItem;

  @Override
  public void storeTop( Item top ) {
    assertFalse( storeTopDone );
    assertSame( expectedTopItem, top );
    storeTopDone = true;
  }

  void setExpectedTopItem( Item expectedTopItem ) {
    this.expectedTopItem = expectedTopItem;
  }

  public void verify() {
    assertTrue( storeTopDone );
  }
}
```

The usage snippet of the following mock looks quite similar to the spy example from the preceding one. However, there are small but mighty differences.

```
  private SessionStorageMock sessionStorage;
  private ItemProviderStub itemProvider;
  private Timeline timeline;

  @Before
  public void setUp() {
    itemProvider = new ItemProviderStub();
    sessionStorage = new SessionStorageMock();
    timeline = new Timeline( itemProvider, sessionStorage );
  }
```

```
@Test
public void fetchFirstItems() {
  itemProvider.addItems( FIRST_ITEM, SECOND_ITEM );
  timeline.setFetchCount( 1 );
  sessionStorage.setExpectedTopItem( SECOND_ITEM );

  timeline.fetchItems();
  List<Item> actual = timeline.getItems();

  sessionStorage.verify();
  [...]
}
```

You can see there is no specification verification regarding the indirect output left in the test. And it seems strange that the usual test structure has been twisted a bit. This is because the verification condition gets specified prior to the exercise phase at the end of the fixture setup (mock configuration). Only the mock invocation check is left in the verify phase.

But in return, a mock provides a precise stacktrace in case behavior verification fails. This can ease problem analysis quite a bit. If you take a look at the spy solution again, you will recognize that a failure trace would point to the verify section of the test only. There would be no information about the line of production code that has actually caused the test to fail.

This is completely different with a mock. The trace would let us exactly identify the position where storeTop was called. Having this information, we could easily set a break point and debug the problematic matter.

If you've completed the previous exercises successfully, you will have no problem to go on and replace our spy with a mock. But writing all this test double types by hand is often a bit tedious. So it's no surprise there are libraries available that simplify double handling considerably. The next section will discuss their assets and drawbacks and look into one of them in more detail.

Increasing efficiency with mock frameworks

While hand-crafting test doubles is a skill each unit tester should be able to master, mock frameworks aim to ease stand-in component creation and configuration. Hence, they profess to make your daily testing work more efficient. But as opinions on these tools are divided, this section will clarify the pros and cons and give some examples of decent usage.

The promised land?

"If all you have is a hammer, everything looks like a nail."

There are a couple of frameworks available claiming to simplify the usage of stand-in components. Unfortunately, these libraries do not always do a good job when it comes to the precise test double terminology, *[GOUL12]*, which we've learned in the previous sections. While JMock, *[JMOCK]*, and EasyMock, *[EASYMO]*, for example, basically generate mocks, Mockito, *[MOCKIT]*, despite its name, is spy centric. Maybe that's why most people talk about *mocking*, regardless of what kind of double they are really using.

Nevertheless, there are indications, *[PRIM13]*, that Mockito has evolved into the preferred tool in that area. This is probably because it provides a good-to-read *fluent interface* API, *[FOWL05]*, that integrates well into the unit test phases, and compensates the drawback of spies mentioned previously by providing detailed verification failure messages.

In general, the frameworks generate configurable test doubles on the fly, using byte code generation. Configuration is done prior to the exercise phase by means of the tool API. This allows us to stub return values and record or verify indirect outputs and interactions easily.

There has been a lot written about whether to use such tools or not. Robert C. Martin, for example, prefers hand-written doubles, *[MART14]*, and Michael Boldischar even considers mocking frameworks harmful, *[BOLD11]*. While the latter is describing just plain *misuse*, looking at the effort we already had to put in our simple hand-written examples earlier, it seems implausible when Martin says, "writing those mocks is trivial", *[MART14]*.

After using crafted doubles myself for years, I was instantly sold to the fluent syntax of stubbing and the intuitive way of verification when discovering Mockito. So basically, I consider it an improvement to get rid of hand-written stand-in components. But to some extent, this is surely in the eye of the beholder.

Even so, it is true that test double tools tempt developers to overdo things. For instance, it can be very easy to replace third-party components, which otherwise might be expensive to create. But this is considered bad practice and Steve Freeman and Nat Pryce explain in detail why you should only mock types that you own, *[FRPR10]*.

Third-party code calls for an abstracting adapter layer and, if heavy weighted, also for integration tests. This gets comprehensible when looking at the `ItemProvider` abstraction of our example. Since we own the adapter, we can replace it safely with a double. If the behavior of the involved third-party code changes, we fix this within the adapter and leave our application code alone.

The second trap one easily walks into is writing tests, where a test double returns another test double. If you come to this point, you should reconsider the design of the code you are working with. Using such train wrecks probably breaks the Law of Demeter, *[WIKILD]*, which means that there might be something wrong with the way your objects are coupled together.

> *"Excited that you can mock everything, huh? Slow down and make sure that you really need to verify interactions. Chances are you don't."*

> – *Tomek Kaczanowski, [KACZ13]*

We've focused in the previous sections on the usage of indirect inputs and outputs in order to achieve proper isolation of the SUT. But we've already noticed that verification of indirect outputs bears the risk of coupling implementation details tightly to a test. This is unfortunate, as it impairs the degrees of freedom available for changing the SUT's internal code. Mock frameworks make it very easy to check for interactions only as well, which is why it is so tempting to use doubles for verification, even if we could do better.

Last but not least, if you think about going with a test double framework, you should keep in mind that this is usually a long-term decision affecting a whole team. It is probably not the best idea to mix different frameworks due to a coherent coding style. Moreover, even if you use only one, consider that each (new) member has to learn the tool specific API.

After this discussion about the pros and cons and proper application of mock frameworks, let's have a look at how their proper usage can simplify our life.

Basic stubbing

In our timeline example, we've introduced the `SessionStorage` collaborator to be able to restore the component's state on program restart. We've seen so far how we could verify that the itemlist's top item gets stored using the indirect output captured by the `storeTop` method of the DOC.

We've already noticed that we need a stub if we want to supply the persistent top item while fetching the first items. But instead of crafting the stub like the `ItemProviderStub`, this time we'll use Mockito to reduce the manual work. The tool provides an API class `Mockito`, which publishes a set of static methods. These serve as an entry point to its capabilities.

When working with the library, it's common practice to use static imports to increase readability. This supports the fluent interface API style, available for configuration or verification of test doubles. The following snippet shows how we create a stand-in component by calling the `mock` method. The method accepts a type token argument and creates an instance of the given type on the fly:

```
SessionStorage storage = mock( SessionStorage.class );
when( storage.readTop() ).thenReturn( SECOND_ITEM );
```

The second line determines that the return value of `readTop` is `SECOND_ITEM` in case the method gets called later on. Again, `when` is a static method provided by the tool's base class. This *when-then* pattern is one of the typical fluently readable constructs used for stub equipment or spy verification.

So let's have a look at our fetch first items scenario to see how we can use Mockito to verify the recovery of a top item. This time we assume that our session store returns an item representing the most recent entry of a previous session. Fetching the first items should reflect this by loading the items starting after the given item.

```
private SessionStorage sessionStorage;
private ItemProviderStub itemProvider;
private Timeline timeline;

@Before
public void setUp() {
  itemProvider = new ItemProviderStub();
  sessionStorage = mock( SessionStorage.class );
  timeline = new Timeline( itemProvider, sessionStorage );
}

@Test
public void fetchFirstItemsWithTopItemToRecover() {
  itemProvider.addItems( FIRST_ITEM, SECOND_ITEM, THIRD_ITEM );
  when( sessionStorage.readTop() ).thenReturn( SECOND_ITEM );
  timeline.setFetchCount( 1 );

  timeline.fetchItems();
  List<Item> actual = timeline.getItems();

  assertEquals( 1, actual.size() );
  assertSame( SECOND_ITEM, actual.get( 0 ) );
  [...]
}
```

Using Mockito allows us to work with the original DOC type instead of special double implementations, which can be particularly neat in cases where we have to deal with class extensions instead of interface implementations. As you can see, we use the when-then pattern to configure our stub during the test's in-line fixture setup. And that's all there is to do.

It is noteworthy that we expect SECOND_ITEM to be the only value to be loaded. This is because we've reduced the fetch-count to a single entry and the second item is the one which was loaded before. So now that you're understanding the basics of stubbing, you'll probably wonder what the item provider might look like if replaced by means of the tool. No problem at all!

```
private SessionStorage sessionStorage;
private ItemProvider itemProvider;
private Timeline timeline;

@Before
public void setUp() {
  itemProvider = mock( ItemProvider.class );
  sessionStorage = mock( SessionStorage.class );
  timeline = new Timeline( itemProvider, sessionStorage );
}

@Test
public void fetchFirstItemsWithTopItemToRecover() {
  when( sessionStorage.readTop() ).thenReturn( SECOND_ITEM );
  when( itemProvider.fetchItems( SECOND_ITEM, 0 ) )
    .thenReturn( emptyList() );
  timeline.setFetchCount( 1 );

  timeline.fetchItems();
  List<Item> actual = timeline.getItems();

  assertEquals( 1, actual.size() );
  assertSame( SECOND_ITEM, actual.get( 0 ) );
  [...]
}
```

You can see in the preceding snippet how we configure the item provider's fetchItems return value to be an empty list. We expect the ancestor to be our SECOND_ITEM. As this represents the first and only list entry, we expect the actual fetchCount parameter to be zero:

```
int actualFetchCount = timeline.getFetchCount() - 1;
```

Although the new version is more slender than the previous one, it is also obvious that it's coupled more tightly to the component internals. Which means the slenderness does not always come for free. If one could think of a different but valid solution using other arguments on `fetchItems`, for example, the new test version would fail. This is important to keep in mind and before putting our component's implementation details into a cast, we might be better off by keeping our hand-crafted half-fake, half-stub double for once.

As a last topic regarding mock frameworks, let's have a look at how verification of indirect output is supported.

Indirect output verification

One of the nice things about Mockito is that the role of how we use our test double instance is not predefined. Well, it always records interactions and is hence, in principle, always a spy, but what the eye does not see, the heart does not grieve over. Meaning, if we use a replacement only to provide indirect input, it simply serves as a stub. This is a bit more complicated with hand-written doubles, in particular when combined with implicit setup.

So it is not astonishing that the double role might vary from test to test. While the `SessionStorage` stand-in performs in `fetchFirstItemsWithTopItemToRecover` as a stub, we could easily use it in another context as a spy. Checking whether a collaborator receives indirect output can be done, as shown in the following line of code:

```
verify( sessionStorage ).storeTop( SECOND_ITEM );
```

Again, the tool's main class provides a static method to start the verification process. The method `verify` takes the spy as a parameter and returns a proxy that allows to check whether the `FIRST_ITEM` has been provided as indirect output. If the argument does not match, an `AssertionError` is thrown. So let's have a look at how we can replace the verify phase of `fetchFirstItems` with a Mockito spy:

```
private SessionStorage sessionStorage;
private ItemProviderStub itemProvider;
private Timeline timeline;

@Before
public void setUp() {
  itemProvider = new ItemProviderStub();
  sessionStorage = mock( SessionStorage.class );
  timeline = new Timeline( itemProvider, sessionStorage );
}

@Test
```

```
public void fetchFirstItems() {
  itemProvider.addItems( FIRST_ITEM, SECOND_ITEM );
  timeline.setFetchCount( 1 );

  timeline.fetchItems();
  List<Item> actual = timeline.getItems();

  verify( sessionStorage ).storeTop( SECOND_ITEM );
  [...]
}
```

As you can see, we expect that loading the first items selects SECOND_ITEM as the top item. Because of this, it is written as an indirect output to our session store. With the built-in recording mechanism of the spy, this is a piece of cake to check. But before concluding this basic introduction, let's have a look at a bit more sophisticated situation. Consider that we need to restore the complete timeline data structure, and to do so, SessionStore would provide a store(Memento) and a read(Memento) method.

The previous approach would not work as the state preserving memento instance is created within our timeline component. The implicit identity check of the previous example is not possible anymore. For such cases, the library provides *matchers*. These can be used to check whether a recorded value fits the expected one. Simple matchers check for equality, containment, or assignment compatibility. For more difficult situations, there is a particular ArgumentCaptor that allows explicit checks on the captured output. The following listing shows how capturing works:

```
ArgumentCaptor<Memento> captor = forClass( Memento.class );
verify( sessionStorage ).store( captor.capture() );
assertTrue( !captor.getValue().getItems().isEmpty() );
```

ArgumentCaptor provides a static method forClass, taking a type token argument to instantiate a parameterized captor. This instance supplies an assignment-compatible matcher when it comes to intercepting the actual output value. Interception is done by calling the method capture, as shown in the preceding listing. While on first sight this looks like magic, it isn't that complicated at all. The method capture returns a matcher that is recognized by the verification proxy, and hence, it is possible to transfer the value of interest to the captor instance. Finally, this value can be accessed with getValue to write appropriate assertions.

Of course, there is much more to know about test double handling with Mockito. But we've covered enough to get an impression of how mock frameworks can facilitate our lives when it comes down to the replacement of DOCs with stand-in components. For more information, please refer to the tool's documentation.

We'll conclude this chapter with another category of classes useful to ease testing.

Using test helpers

Besides components, collaborators, data types, and test cases, we occasionally need another category of classes to write our tests efficiently. These utility classes provide any kind of testing related functionality that we want to reuse in several tests. This section explains some of the common practices.

Motivation

While writing tests, we'll inevitably find ourselves in a situation were we'll code the same routine for fixture setup, verification, or the like. If this happens to be in the same test case, we can extract a method for common usage. But sometimes, we could also make use of these methods in other test classes.

Java provides class inheritance, and so it's possible to introduce a common super type supplying these helping methods. After that, a particular test case can extend from this type and reuse the testing related functionality. Problem solved, right?

Wrong! First of all, inheritance is more than what the compiler checks. Class hierarchies represent **abstract data types** (**ADT**) that follow specific rules with respect to generalization and specialization. So usually, there are preconditions, class invariants, and post-conditions that need to be met when inheriting an ADT's behavior. This is also known as the **Liskov Substitution Principle**.

Although it's possible to whitewash oneself a super type of test case into an ADT definition, inheritance has another restriction that finally downs this approach. For good reason, the Java language has no support for multi-inheritance at the class level. This implies that we'll, sooner or later, have to mix in different concerns into one super-duper test case, which will eventually end up in a mess.

So normally, this isn't the way to go. Instead, we'll provide separate helper classes that care about a single concern. Tests delegate to the functionality made available by those utility types, which keeps our test class structure clean and flexible.

If you are working with multiple modules in your project, it is not unusual that you need specific test utilities in more than one of them. Instead of introducing non-natural module-dependencies to the one in which the helper originated, it is preferable to initiate a test utility module as a common place for such types.

A *test helper* publishes its functionality either by class or instance methods, rarely as a mix of both. The following sections examine the general idea of the different approaches, as denoted by *Meszaros*, *[MESZ07]*.

The test helper class

If all the utility methods of a test helper are stateless, a unit test needs no particular instance to be able to incorporate the provided functionality. Typical use cases are common create — or delegate — methods for fixture setup and/or teardown, summarizing of particular assertions, or facilitation of indirect exercise invocations.

The latter might be necessary when testing components that rely on an external trigger to perform a desired functionality. Think of an example of a UI widget compound expecting a button to be pressed by a user. If you are lucky, an API for programmatic release of such an events exists, but even then, this often comes along with writing a lot of boilerplate.

A test helper can reduce such boilerplate considerably, and improve readability by providing, for example, a fluent interface API. Although UI component tests are technically at the borderline to integration tests, let's continue the thought and see how this could look like in practice.

Consider that we are about to write a **Standard Widget Toolkit [SWT]**-based GUI for our timeline model. More precisely, we need to check the proper invocation of the functionality deposited with the fetch-new-items button. While developing UI component tests, you need to do such things all the time. Luckily, we can resort to a publicly available test helper, *[APPE14]*. The SWTEventHelper provides a static trigger method that expects the event type you want to issue as an argument:

```
@Test
public void fetchNew() {
  TimelineUi timelineUi = ...

  trigger( SWT.Selection ).on( timelineUi.fetchNew );

  // verify collaborators have been invoked properly for example
}
```

To be able to invoke the event on the responsible UI widget, TimelineUi opens encapsulation a bit and allows access to the button responsible for triggering the fetch new operation. We do this by increasing the button's visibility to package private (see *Chapter 1, Getting Started*). Note how the fluently readable test helper API accepts the button with the on statement.

Sometimes, stateless operations are not enough, which is why we conclude this chapter discussing the nature of stateful utility classes.

The test helper object

Test helpers providing instances are helpful to swap out more complex collaborators or data graphs into a root object, which allows coherent initialization and disposal. While this indicates usage in the context of fixture setup and teardown, such instances may also be useful for creating high-order assertions.

A particular test helper object pattern is the *object mother* that may consist of one or more test helpers with common creation, configuration, and/or teardown methods. A test uses a combination of these methods to set up its ready-to-use fixture objects, *[MESZ07]*.

In *Chapter 6, Reducing Boilerplate with JUnit Rules*, you'll learn about a JUnit feature that allows to plug a test helper instance around a test's life cycle. This eases and secures, in equal measure, the helper's usage since necessary teardown steps are performed automatically.

It's notable that test helper introduction isn't always motivated by reuse. Sometimes, it is advisable to encapsulate and externalize certain setup functionality merely to increase readability by condensing the test class code to the crucial stuff.

If we look at our timeline test, it might happen that component and collaborator initialization methods get too mingled and confusing. So it might help to introduce an object mother to reduce the glue code a bit. However, before doing so, ensure that your component isn't dealing with too many concerns and respects the single responsibility principle. If it doesn't, it would be better to split up the component instead.

Well, this was quite a chapter, so let's summarize what we've learned before reading on.

Summary

In this chapter, we've seen how collaborating components have an impact on our ability to write tests that run units shielded from the influences of other parts of a software system. We've learned how to use test doubles to isolate the components from real-world DOCs and hence, keep our tests fast, reliable, and maintainable.

To do so, you've been pointed first to the significance of indirect inputs and outputs. Once you understood this basic interaction principle between SUT and DOC, we went on with an in-depth discussion of the various double patterns available. In this context, you've been told about the intended use of dummy-, fake-, stub, spy, and mock stand-in types. After looking at the possibilities of mock frameworks and questioning their pros and cons, you experienced how generated doubles increase work efficiency in practice.

Finally, you learned about test helpers that, in contrast with doubles, do not collaborate with components under test, but rather decouple the test cases and fixture handling by extracting common functionality. Overall, the knowledge and skills that you've acquired in this chapter will give you a comprehensive set of techniques to face the challenges of unit testing in real-world scenarios.

The next chapter will build upon what you've learned so far, and look into situations that deal with particular boundary conditions. Essentially, it'll teach you to write tests that verify exceptional flow.

4
Testing Exceptional Flow

Special care has to be taken when testing a component's functionality under exception-raising conditions. In this chapter, you'll learn how to use the various capture and verification possibilities and discuss their pros and cons. As robust software design is one of the declared goals of the test-first approach, we're going to see how tests intertwine with the fail fast strategy on selected boundary conditions. Finally, we're going to conclude with an in-depth explanation of working with collaborators under exceptional flow and see how stubbing of exceptional behavior can be achieved. The topics covered in this chapter are as follows:

- Testing patterns
- Treating collaborators

Testing patterns

Testing exceptional flow is a bit trickier than verifying the outcome of normal execution paths. The following section will explain why and introduce the different techniques available to get this job done.

Using the fail statement

"Always expect the unexpected"

– Adage based on Heraclitus

Testing corner cases often results in the necessity to verify that a functionality throws a particular exception. Think, for example, of a `java.util.List` implementation. It quits the retrieval attempt of a list's element by means of a non-existing index number with `java.lang.ArrayIndexOutOfBoundsException`.

Working with exceptional flow is somewhat special as without any precautions, the exercise phase would terminate immediately. But this is not what we want since it eventuates in a test failure. Indeed, the exception itself is the expected outcome of the behavior we want to check.

From this, it follows that we have to capture the exception before we can verify anything. As we all know, we do this in Java with a `try-catch` construct. The `try` block contains the actual invocation of the functionality we are about to test. The catch `block` again allows us to get a grip on the expected outcome — the exception thrown during the exercise.

 Note that we usually keep our hands off `Error`, so we confine the angle of view in this book to exceptions.

So far so good, but we have to bring up to our minds that in case no exception is thrown, this has to be classified as misbehavior. Consequently, the test has to fail. JUnit's built-in assertion capabilities provide the `org.junit.Assert.fail` method, which can be used to achieve this. The method unconditionally throws an instance of `java.lang.AssertionError` if called.

The classical approach of testing exceptional flow with JUnit adds a `fail` statement straight after the functionality invocation within the `try` block. The idea behind is that this statement should never be reached if the SUT behaves correctly. But if not, the assertion error marks the test as failed.

It is self-evident that capturing should narrow down the expected exception as much as possible. Do not catch `IOException` if you expect `FileNotFoundException`, for example. Unintentionally thrown exceptions must pass the catch block unaffected, lead to a test failure and, therefore, give you a good hint for troubleshooting with their stack trace.

We insinuated earlier in this book that the fetch-count range check of our timeline example would probably be better off throwing `IllegalArgumentException` on boundary violations. Let's have a look at how we can change the `setFetchCountExceedsLowerBound` test to verify different behaviors with the try-catch exception testing pattern (see the following listing):

```java
@Test
public void setFetchCountExceedsLowerBound() {
  int tooSmall = Timeline.FETCH_COUNT_LOWER_BOUND - 1;

  try {
    timeline.setFetchCount( tooSmall );
    fail();
```

```
    } catch( IllegalArgumentException actual ) {
      String message = actual.getMessage();
      String expected
        = format( Timeline.ERROR_EXCEEDS_LOWER_BOUND, tooSmall );
      assertEquals( expected, message );
      assertTrue( message.contains( valueOf( tooSmall ) ) );
    }
  }
}
```

It can be clearly seen how setFetchCount, the functionality under test, is called within the try block, directly followed by a fail statement. The caught exception is narrowed down to the expected type. The test avails of the inline fixture setup to initialize the exceeds-lower-bound value in the tooSmall local variable because it is used more than once.

The verification checks that the thrown message matches an expected one. Our test calculates the expectation with the aid of java.lang.String.format (static import) based on the same pattern, which is also used internally by the timeline to produce the text. Once again, we loosen encapsulation a bit to ensure that the malicious value gets mentioned correctly. Purists may prefer only the String.contains variant, which, on the other hand would be less accurate.

Although this works fine, it looks pretty ugly and is not very readable. Besides, it blurs a bit the separation of the exercise and verification phases, and so it is no wonder that there have been other techniques invented for exception testing.

Annotated expectations

After the arrival of annotations in the Java language, JUnit got a thorough overhauling. We already mentioned the @Test type used to mark a particular method as an executable test. To simplify exception testing, it has been given the expected attribute. This defines that the anticipated outcome of a unit test should be an exception and it accepts a subclass of Throwable to specify its type.

Running a test of this kind captures exceptions automatically and checks whether the caught type matches the specified one. The following snippet shows how this can be used to validate that our timeline constructor doesn't accept null as the injection parameter:

```
@Test( expected = IllegalArgumentException.class )
public void constructWithNullAsItemProvider() {
  new Timeline( null, mock( SessionStorage.class ) );
}
```

Here, we've got a test, the body statements of which merge setup and exercise in one line for compactness. Although the verification result is specified ahead of the method's signature definition, of course, it gets evaluated at last. This means that the runtime test structure isn't twisted. But it is a bit of a downside from the readability point of view as it breaks the usual test format.

However, the approach bears a real risk when using it in more complex scenarios. The next listing shows an alternative of setFetchCountExceedsLowerBound using the expected attribute:

```
@Test( expected = IllegalArgumentException.class )
public void setFetchCountExceedsLowerBound() {
  Timeline timeline = new Timeline( null, null );

  timeline.setFetchCount( Timeline.FETCH_COUNT_LOWER_BOUND - 1 );
}
```

On the face of it, this might look fine because the test run would succeed apparently with a green bar. But given that the timeline constructor already throws IllegalArgumentException due to the initialization with null, the virtual point of interest is never reached. So any setFetchCount implementation will pass this test. This renders it not only useless, but it even lulls you into a false sense of security!

Certainly, the approach is most hazardous when checking for runtime exceptions because they can be thrown undeclared. Thus, they can emerge practically everywhere and overshadow the original test intention unnoticed. Not being able to validate the state of the thrown exception narrows down the reasonable operational area of this concept to simple use cases, such as the constructor parameter verification mentioned previously.

Finally, here are two more remarks on the initial example. First, it might be debatable whether IllegalArgumentException is appropriate for an argument-not-null-check from a design point of view. But as this discussion is as old as the hills and probably will never be settled, we won't argue about that. IllegalArgumentException was favored over NullPointerException basically because it seemed to be an evident way to build up a comprehensible example. To specify a different behavior of the tested use case, one simply has to define another Throwable type as the expected value.

Second, as a side effect, the test shows how a generated test double can make our life much easier. You've probably already noticed that the session storage stand-in created on the fly serves as a dummy. This is quite nice as we don't have to implement one manually and as it decouples the test from storage-related signatures, which may break the test in future when changing. But keep in mind that such a created-on-the-fly dummy lacks the implicit no-operation-check we've planted into our crafted one in the preceding chapter. Hence, this approach might be too fragile under some circumstances.

With annotations being too brittle for most usage scenarios and the try-fail-catch pattern being too crabbed, JUnit provides a special test helper called `ExpectedException`, which we'll take a look at now.

Verification with the ExpectedException rule

The third possibility offered to verify exceptions is the `ExpectedException` class. This type belongs to a special category of test utilities we'll cover in *Chapter 6, Reducing Boilerplate with JUnit Rules*. For the moment, it is sufficient to know that rules allow us to embed a test method into custom pre- and post-operations at runtime.

In doing so, the expected exception helper can catch the thrown instance and perform the appropriate verifications. A rule has to be defined as a nonstatic public field, annotated with `@Rule`, as shown in the following `TimelineTest` excerpt. See how the rule object gets set up implicitly here with a factory method:

```
public class TimelineTest {

  @Rule
  public ExpectedException thrown = ExpectedException.none();

  [...]

  @Test
  public void setFetchCountExceedsUpperBound() {
    int tooLargeValue = FETCH_COUNT_UPPER_BOUND + 1;
    thrown.expect( IllegalArgumentException.class );
    thrown.expectMessage( valueOf( tooLargeValue ) );

    timeline.setFetchCount( tooLargeValue );
  }

  [...]
}
```

Compared to the try-fail-catch approach, the code is easier to read and write. The helper instance supports several methods to specify the anticipated outcome. Apart from the static imports of constants used for compactness, this specification reproduces pretty much the same validations as the original test. `ExpectedExcepti on#expectedMessage` expects a substring of the actual message in case you wonder, and we omitted the exact formatting here for brevity.

In case the exercise phase of `setFetchCountExceedsUpperBound` does not throw an exception, the rule ensures that the test fails. In this context, it is about time we mentioned the utility's factory method `none`. Its name indicates that as long as no expectations are configured, the helper assumes that a test run should terminate normally. This means that no artificial fail has to be issued. This way, a mix of standard and exceptional flow tests can coexist in one and the same test case.

Even so, the test helper has to be configured prior to the exercise phase, which still leaves room for improvement with respect to canonizing the test structure. As we'll see next, the possibility of Java 8 to compact closures into lambda expressions enables us to write even leaner and cleaner structured exceptional flow tests.

Capturing exceptions with closures

When writing tests, we strive to end up with a clear representation of separated test phases in the correct order. All of the previous approaches for testing exceptional flow did more or less a poor job in this regard. Looking once more at the classical try-fail-catch pattern, we recognize, however, that it comes closest.

It strikes us that if we put some work into it, we can extract exception capturing into a reusable utility method. This method would accept a functional interface—the representation of the exception-throwing functionality under test—and return the caught exception.

The `ThrowableCaptor` test helper puts the idea into practice:

```
public class ThrowableCaptor {

  @FunctionalInterface
  public interface Actor {
    void act() throws Throwable;
  }

  public static Throwable thrownBy( Actor actor ) {
    try {
      actor.act();
    } catch( Throwable throwable ) {
      return throwable;
```

```
        }
    return null;
    }
}
```

We see the `Actor` interface that serves as a functional callback. It gets executed within a `try` block of the `thrownBy` method. If an exception is thrown, which should be the normal path of execution, it gets caught and returned as the result. Bear in mind that we have omitted the `fail` statement of the original try-fail-catch pattern. We consider the capturer as a helper for the exercise phase. Thus, we merely return `null` if no exception is thrown and leave it to the afterworld to deal correctly with the situation.

How capturing using this helper in combination with a lambda expression works is shown by the next variant of `setFetchCountExceedsUpperBound`, and this time, we've achieved the clear phase separation we're in search of:

```
@Test
public void setFetchCountExceedsUpperBound() {
    int tooLarge = FETCH_COUNT_UPPER_BOUND + 1;

    Throwable actual
        = thrownBy( ()-> timeline.setFetchCount( tooLarge ) );

    String message = actual.getMessage();
    assertNotNull( actual );
    assertTrue( actual instanceof IllegalArgumentException );
    assertTrue( message.contains( valueOf( tooLarge ) ) );
    assertEquals( format( ERROR_EXCEEDS_UPPER_BOUND, tooLarge ),
                message );
}
```

Please note that we've added an additional not-null-check compared to the verifications of the previous version. We do this as a replacement for the non-existing failure enforcement. Indeed, the following `instanceof` check would fail implicitly if `actual` was `null`. But this would also be misleading since it overshadows the true failure reason. Stating that `actual` must not be `null` points out clearly the expected post condition that has not been met.

In *Chapter 7, Improving Readability with Custom Assertions*, you'll learn about alternative ways to write test verifications. One of the libraries presented there will be AssertJ. The latter is mainly intended to improve validation expressions. But it also provides a test helper, which supports the closure pattern you've just learned to make use of. Another choice to avoid writing your own helper could be the library Fishbowl, *[FISBOW]*.

Now that we understand the available testing patterns, let's discuss a few system-spanning aspects when dealing with exceptional flow in practice.

Treating collaborators

Considerations we've made in *Chapter 3, Developing Independently Testable Units,* about how a software system can be built upon collaborating components, foreshadows that we have to take good care when modelling our overall strategy for exceptional flow. Because of this, we'll start this section with an introduction of the fail fast strategy, which is a perfect match to the test-first approach. The second part of the section will show you how to deal with checked exceptions thrown by collaborators.

Fail fast

Until now, we've learned that exceptions can serve in corner cases as an expected outcome, which we need to verify with tests. As an example, we've changed the behavior of our timeline fetch-count setter. The new version throws `IllegalArgumentException` if the given parameter is out of range. While we've explained how to test this, you may have wondered whether throwing an exception is actually an improvement.

On the contrary, you might think, doesn't the exception make our program more fragile as it bears the risk of an ugly error popping up or even of crashing the entire application? Aren't those things we want to prevent by all means? So, wouldn't it be better to stick with the old version and silently ignore arguments that are out of range?

At first sight, this may sound reasonable, but doing so is ostrich-like head-in-the-sand behavior. According to the motto: if we can't see them, they aren't there, and so, they can't hurt us. Ignoring an input that is obviously wrong can lead to misbehavior of our software system later on. The reason for the problem is probably much harder to track down compared to an immediate failure.

Generally speaking, this practice disconnects the effects of a problem from its cause. As a consequence, you often have to deal with stack traces leading to dead ends or worse. Consider, for example, that we'd initialize the timeline fetch-count as an invariant employed by a constructor argument. Moreover, the value we use would be negative and silently ignored by the component. In addition, our application would make some item position calculations based on this value.

Sure enough, the calculation results would be faulty. If we're lucky, an exception would be thrown, when, for example, trying to access a particular item based on these calculations. However, the given stack trace would reveal nothing about the reason that originally led to the situation. However, if we're unlucky, the misbehavior will not be detected until the software has been released to end users.

On the other hand, with the new version of `setFetchCount`, this kind of translocated problem can never occur. A failure trace would point directly to the initial programming mistake, hence avoiding follow-up issues. This means failing immediately and visibly increases robustness due to short feedback cycles and pertinent exceptions. Jim Shore has given this design strategy the name fail fast, *[SHOR04]*.

Shore points out that the heart of fail fast are assertions. Similar to the JUnit assert statements, an assertion fails on a condition that isn't met. Typical assertions might be not-null-checks, in-range-checks, and so on. But how do we decide if it's necessary to fail fast? While assertions of input arguments are apparently a potential use case scenario, checking of return values or invariants may also be so. Sometimes, such conditions are described in code comments, such as *// foo should never be null because...,* which is a clear indication that suggests to replace the note with an appropriate assertion. See the next snippet demonstrating the principle:

```
public void doWithAssert() {
  [...]
  boolean condition = ...; // check some invariant
  if( !condition ) {
    throw new IllegalStateException( "Condition not met." )
  }
  [...]
}
```

But be careful not to overdo things because in most cases, code will fail fast by default. So, you don't have to include a not-null-check after each and every variable assignment for example. Such paranoid programming styles decrease readability for no value-add at all.

A last point to consider is your overall exception-handling strategy. The intention of assertions is to reveal programming or configuration mistakes as early as possible. Because of this, we strictly make use of runtime exception types only. Catching exceptions at random somewhere up the call stack of course thwarts the whole purpose of this approach. So, beware of the absurd try-catch-log pattern that you often see scattered all over the code of scrubs, and which is demonstrated in the next listing as a deterrent only:

```
private Data readSomeData() {
  try {
```

```
      return source.readData();
   } catch( Exception hardLuck ) {
      // NEVER DO THIS!
      hardLuck.printStackTrace();
   }
   return null;
}
```

The sample code projects exceptional flow to `null` return values and disguises the fact that something seriously went wrong. It surely does not get better using a logging framework or even worse, by swallowing the exception completely. Analysis of an error by means of stack trace logs is cumbersome and often fault-prone. In particular, this approach usually leads to logs jammed with ignored traces, where one more or less does not attract attention. In such an environment, it's like looking for a needle in a haystack when trying to find out why a follow-up problem occurs.

Instead, use the central exception handling mechanism at reasonable boundaries. You can create a bottom level exception handler around a GUI's message loop. Ensure that background threads report problems appropriately or secure event notification mechanisms for example. Otherwise, you shouldn't bother with exception handling in your code. As outlined in the next paragraph, securing resource management with try-finally should most of the time be sufficient.

The stubbing of exceptional behavior

Every now and then, we come across collaborators, which declare checked exceptions in some or all of their method signatures. There is a debate going on for years now whether or not checked exceptions are evil, *[HEVEEC]*. However, in our daily work, we simply can't elude them as they pop up in adapters around third-party code or get burnt in legacy code we aren't able to change. So, what are the options we have in these situations?

> *"It is funny how people think that the important thing about exceptions is handling them. That's not the important thing about exceptions. In a well-written application there's a ratio of ten to one, in my opinion, of try finally to try catch."*
>
> *– Anders Hejlsberg, [HEVEEC]*

Cool. This means that we also declare the exception type in question on our own method signature and let someone else up on the call stack solve the tricky things, right? Although it makes life easier for us for at the moment, acting like this is probably not the brightest idea. If everybody follows that strategy, the higher we get on the stack, the more exception types will occur.

This doesn't scale well and even worse, it exposes details from the depths of the call hierarchy. Because of this, people sometimes simplify things by declaring `java.lang.Exception` as thrown type. Indeed, this gets them rid of the throws declaration tail. But it's also a pauper's oath as it reduces the Java type concept to absurdity.

Fair enough. So, we're presumably better off when dealing with checked exceptions as soon as they occur. But hey, wouldn't this contradict Hejlsberg's statement? And what shall we do with the gatecrasher, meaning is there always a reasonable handling approach? Fortunately there is, and it absolutely conforms with the quote and the preceding fail fast discussion. We envelope the caught checked exception into an appropriate runtime exception, which we afterwards throw instead.

This way, every caller of our component's functionality can use it without worrying about exception handling. If necessary, it is sufficient to use a try-finally block to ensure the disposal or closure of open resources for example. As described previously, we leave exception handling to bottom line handlers around the message loop or the like.

Now that we know what we have to do, the next question is how can we achieve this with tests? Luckily, with the knowledge about stubs learned in the previous chapter, you're almost there. Normally handling a checked exception represents a boundary condition. We can regard the thrown exception as an indirect input to our SUT. All we have to do is let the stub throw an expected exception (precondition) and check if the envelope gets delivered properly (postcondition).

For better understanding, let's comprehend the steps in our timeline example. We consider for this section that our `SessionStorage` collaborator declares `IOException` on its methods for any reason whatsoever. The storage interface is shown in the next listing.

```java
public interface SessionStorage {
    void storeTop( Item top ) throws IOException;
    Item readTop() throws IOException;
}
```

Next, we'll have to write a test that reflects our thoughts. At first, we create an `IOException` instance that will serve as an indirect input. Looking at the next snippet, you can see how we configure our storage stub to throw this instance on a call to `storeTop`. As the method does not return anything, the Mockito stubbing pattern looks a bit different than earlier. This time, it starts with the expectation definition. In addition, we use Mockito's `any` matcher, which defines the exception that should be thrown for those calls to `storeTop`, where the given argument is assignment-compatible with the specified type token.

After this, we're ready to exercise the `fetchItems` method and capture the actual outcome. We expect it to be an instance of `IllegalStateException` just to keep things simple. See how we verify that the caught exception wraps the original cause and that the message matches a predefined constant on our component class:

```
@Test
public void fetchItemWithExceptionOnStoreTop()
  throws IOException
{

  IOException cause = new IOException();
  doThrow( cause ).when( storage ).storeTop( any( Item.class ) );

  Throwable actual = thrownBy( () -> timeline.fetchItems() );

  assertNotNull( actual );
  assertTrue( actual instanceof IllegalStateException );
  assertSame( cause, actual.getCause() );
  assertEquals( Timeline.ERROR_STORE_TOP, actual.getMessage() );
}
```

With the test in place, the implementation is pretty easy. Let's assume that we have the item storage extracted to a private timeline method named `storeTopItem`. It gets called somewhere down the road of `fetchItem` and again calls a private method, `getTopItem`. Fixing the compile errors, we end up with a `try-catch` block because we have to deal with `IOException` thrown by `storeTop`. Our first error handling should be empty to ensure that our test case actually fails. The following snippet shows the ultimate version, which will make the test finally pass:

```
static final String ERROR_STORE_TOP
  = "Unable to save top item";

[...]

private void storeTopItem() {
  try {
    sessionStorage.storeTop( getTopItem() );
  } catch( IOException cause ) {
```

```
        throw new IllegalStateException( ERROR_STORE_TOP, cause );
    }
}
```

Of course, real-world situations can sometimes be more challenging, for example, when the collaborator throws a mix of checked and runtime exceptions. At times, this results in tedious work. But if the same type of wrapping exception can always be used, the implementation can often be simplified. First, re-throw all runtime exceptions; second, catch exceptions by their common super type and re-throw them embedded within a wrapping runtime exception (the following listing shows the principle):

```
private void storeTopItem() {
    try {
        sessionStorage.storeTop( getTopItem() );
    } catch( RuntimeException rte ) {
        throw rte;
    } catch( Exception cause ) {
        throw new IllegalStateException( ERROR_STORE_TOP, cause );
    }
}
```

Summary

In this chapter, you learned how to validate the proper behavior of an SUT with respect to exceptional flow. You experienced how to apply the various capture and verification options, and we discussed their strengths and weaknesses. Supplementary to the test-first approach, you were taught the concepts of the fail fast design strategy and recognized how adapting it increases the overall robustness of applications. Last but not least, we explained how to handle collaborators that throw checked exceptions and how to stub their exceptional bearing.

In the next chapter, we'll discuss how exchangeable JUnit processor types allow us to adjust the environment of a test to specific requirements. We'll explain the tool runners architecture and introduce some of the more useful implementations.

5
Using Runners for Particular Testing Purposes

Until now, we used test cases as the pivotal point in writing self-checking behavior specifications of components. But they can serve other purposes, such as collecting particular test classes to run them as a group too, since pluggable processors allow execution adjustments to highly diverse demands. This chapter will start by explaining the architecture behind this mechanism and advance, for a profound understanding, with what it takes to write a custom extension. With these insights, we'll be ready to discuss a couple of valuable use cases and also draw attention to some tradeoffs. Since one of the most important applications is parameterized tests, we will cover the available approaches thoroughly in the last section. The topics we are going to look at briefly include:

- Understanding the architecture
- Using custom runners
- Writing dataset tests

Understanding the architecture

Although we've already encountered quite a few of JUnit's essential testing capabilities, there is more than meets the eye. Beyond standard test execution, it is possible to meet other requirements by means of pluggable test processors. The first section of this chapter will explain the most relevant concepts and deepen our knowledge by developing a basic extension.

What are runners good for?

"If you get stuck, draw with a different pen. Change your tools; it may free your thinking."

– Paul Arden

In the previous chapters, we heard a good deal about unit testing with respect to structure and isolation. These concepts are well supported by the default behavior of JUnit. However, sometimes, there are scenarios that demand additional or different capabilities. Imagine, for example, a set of test cases comprising the specification of a subsystem that should be grouped together for aggregated test runs. You can even consider the need for a special test execution strategy facilitating parameterized test methods.

On that account, the tool offers the adaption of various test processor types. Using this mechanism is reasonable if there is a need for particular test class instantiation, individual test lookup, or different execution behavior. For less fundamental amendments, there is a more lightweight possibility, which we will describe in *Chapter 6, Reducing Boilerplate with JUnit Rules*.

Processors are configured individually at the test case level using the `@RunWith` annotation. If this annotation is missing, the `BlockJUnit4ClassRunner` processor is the default choice. This is where the tool's standard behavior comes from. The following snippet shows a declaration, which is equivalent to the preset:

```
@RunWith( BlockJUnit4ClassRunner.class )
public class TimelineTest {
  [...]
}
```

`@RunWith` takes a class reference as argument. An instance of the given type will do the actual test processing. To meet the tool's execution policy, such a type has to be a subclass of `org.junit.runner.Runner`. This explains the suffix of the default's name. Providing a different runner is as simple as changing the declaration's parameter value.

Thus, we've learned that test processors are pluggable. But how does it work exactly?

Looking at the big picture

A runner has to implement two methods of defining the cooperation policy with the tool's runtime instance. The first, `getDescription`, is inherited from its super interface `Describable` and returns an instance of `Description`. A description is used to provide human-readable information about a test, which is to be run or has been run. It can describe a single test (atomic) or a hierarchy of tests (compound). The information provided by each runner is used, for example, by a GUI to depict all tests that a particular launch affects.

The second method is called `run` and takes `RunNotifier` as argument. This is, of course, where all the action happens. Here, the runner is supposed to select the executables of a test case, invoke them, and report the appropriate state information using the notifier callback. We'll provide more insight into this in a minute, when we write our own implementation.

`Runner` has to be an abstract class as it supplies the convenient `testCount` method. The latter provides the number of tests to be run calculated on the information returned by `getDescription`. This enables subclasses to override computation for unusual demands but probably only seldom makes sense. At any rate, this base class is the way to go if you need functionality that differs significantly from the common use cases.

More likely though is that one will extend `ParentRunner<T>`, a subclass of `Runner`. This implements the policy described earlier by delegating a few abstract methods. Essentially, an inheritor works on a list of children. A child is of the generic type `T`. The list of `T` might be the tests defined by a single test case. It should be derived from the constructor-injected test class. Development needs are reduced to retrieve this list of children and to provide the description and execution of a single child.

The `ParentRunner` class itself is responsible among other things for invoking the `@BeforeClass` and `@AfterClass` annotated methods, creating a composite description, and running children sequentially. The annotations are meant to share expensive fixture setups among the children, thus the marked methods get only called once, namely after the entirety of child executions.

We're already aware of the `BlockJUnit4ClassRunner` extension, which is used as the standard JUnit test case processor. The following diagram also contains another extension called `Suite` that we'll cover in the second section of this chapter:

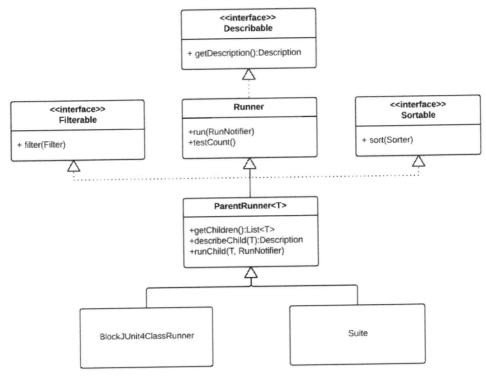

Runner hierarchy

Other than the ones mentioned, the class hierarchy contains two interfaces declaring filtering and sorting capabilities implemented by the parent runner. But before we lose ourselves in too many boring architectural details, let's put some flesh on the bones and see what it takes to develop a simple `Runner`.

Writing your own extension

To get a better feel of the interplay between a runner and its environment, this section outlines how to write a basic extension. We expect our solution to pick up executable methods by a distinct annotation. Hence, we declare an appropriate @ `Execute` type, as shown in the next listing:

```
@Retention( RetentionPolicy.RUNTIME )
@Target( { ElementType.METHOD } )
public @interface Execute {}
```

Nothing surprising here, so we can move swiftly to the chief character that makes use of it. The next `Executor` implementation provides a constructor taking a `Class` parameter. Although this isn't enforced by the super type, the framework expects this signature. The given argument is a type defining the executables we want to run. As you can see, JUnit provides the `TestClass` helper, simplifying certain tasks, such as parsing the contemplable methods.

Next, we supply the `getDescription` functionality, also based on this helper. The actual return value is a compound of the test type information (`createClassDescription`) and its executables (`createMethodDescription`). `Description` provides several factory methods for this purpose.

 Note that `createSuiteDescription` and `createTestDescription` are used with static imports for compactness.

What remains is the realization of the `run` behavior. We solve this by processing the available annotated methods separately. Each execution call uses a newly created test type instance for proper isolation and is invoked within a try-catch construct. Note how the notifier callback instance is used to inform the framework about progress and failures:

```
public class Executor extends Runner {

  private final List<FrameworkMethod> methods;
  private final TestClass meta;

  public Executor( Class<?> testType ) {
    meta = new TestClass( testType );
    methods = meta.getAnnotatedMethods( Execute.class );
  }

  @Override
  public Description getDescription() {
    Description result = createClassDescription();
    methods.forEach( method
      -> result.addChild( createMethodDescription( method )
    ) );
    return result;
  }

  @Override
  public void run( RunNotifier notifier ) {
    methods.forEach( method -> run( notifier, method ) );
```

```
    }

    private void run( RunNotifier notifier, FrameworkMethod method ) {
      Description description = createMethodDescription( method );
      notifier.fireTestStarted( description );
      try {
        Object target = meta.getJavaClass().newInstance();
        method.invokeExplosively( target );
      } catch( Throwable problem ) {
        Failure failure = new Failure( description, problem );
        notifier.fireTestFailure( failure );
      }
      notifier.fireTestFinished( description );
    }

    private Description createClassDescription() {
      String name = meta.getName();
      Execute annotations = meta.getAnnotation( Execute.class );
      return createSuiteDescription( name, annotations );
    }

    private Description createMethodDescription(
      FrameworkMethod method )
    {
      return createTestDescription( meta.getClass(),
        method.getName() );
    }
  }
}
```

Despite this `Runner` extension being anything but production ready, it's sufficient to get a basic sample working. `ExecutorSample`, which is used in the next code, configures our runner using the `@RunWith` annotation. The class contains three methods constituting the different results an execution could lead to. The first method is rated as a success, the second as an error, and the third as a failure. Please affirm to understand how these results are picked up by the executor's run method and how they get reported to the JUnit environment:

```
@RunWith( Executor.class )
public class ExecutorSample {

  @Execute
  public void doIt() {}

  @Execute
  public void doItWithProblem() {
```

```
      throw new RuntimeException( "Bad" );
  }

  @Execute
  public void doItWithFailure() {
    throw new AssertionError( "Invalid" );
  }
}
```

Believe it or not, that's all we need to be ready to launch the sample from within the IDE. The following screenshot displays the result of such a run. You can see clearly how the single tests are marked with different overlay images according to their respective outcomes. Regard also how the selected failure trace reflects the assertion message of doItWithFailure. We are delighted to see that the stack trace proves that it was actually an Executor instance that processed ExecutorSample.

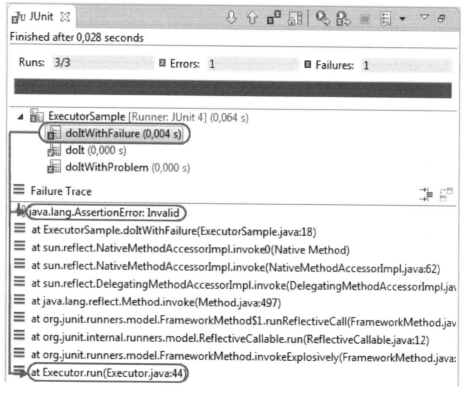

Executor launch

Now that we've got a sufficient comprehension of what runners are good for and how they work, let's have a look at a few more useful implementations.

Using custom runners

This section will introduce different extensions that are helpful for structuring your test universe. Further, we'll shed some light on the consequences of overdone runner usage.

Furnishing a suite with test cases

Probably one of the best known runners is `Suite`. Its purpose is to compose several test cases and/or other suites into a single entity that is processable by JUnit, which allows an example to combine all test cases of a subsystem. This might be an appropriate excerpt with respect to the overall test execution duration on your local machine—if you're about to enhance some of the subsystem's capabilities.

The suite-defining class has normally no body implementation. The composition is accomplished by means of the `@SuiteClasses` annotation, which is used to specify a list of test cases or nested suites:

```
@RunWith( Suite.class )
@SuiteClasses( {
  TimelineTest.class,
  UiITest.class,
  [...]
} )
public class AllTestSuite {}
```

The `AllTestSuite` example illustrates how to configure the processor and the list of test cases designated to be executed on suite launch.

Structuring suites into categories

The structuring capabilities of suites are somewhat limited. Because of this, JUnit 4.8 introduced the `Categories` runner, which is still classified as experimental. To begin with, you declare custom category types, such as unit, integration, and acceptance tests in the form of marker interfaces. A test case or method is assigned to one of those with the aid of the `@Category` annotation. Consider the following category declarations:

```
public interface Unit {}
public interface Integration {}
public interface Acceptance {}
```

We want our `TimelineTest` case to belong to the category `Unit`, so we make use of the `Category` annotation:

```
@Category(Unit.class)
public class TimelineTest {
  [...]
}
```

Since `Categories` is an extension of `Suite`, it enables us, by means of `@SuiteClasses`, to incorporate `AllTestSuite` defined previously. Additionally, it provides include and/or exclude declarations to filter the overall collection of tests:

```
@RunWith( Categories.class )
@IncludeCategory( Unit.class )
@SuiteClasses( {
  AllTestSuite.class,
} )
public class AllUnitTestSuite {}
```

The `AllUnitTestSuite` example shows how the selection of tests to execute is restricted to those that are assigned to the `Unit` category. But keep in mind that `Category` is not confined to class-level declarations only and also accepts multiple category values.

Concluding this topic, it may be worth noting that it is possible to configure filters based on category assignments in Maven or Gradle build configuration files directly, without the need to define particular category classes.

 For more information about this, please refer to the Categories section of the JUnit online documentation at `https://github.com/junit-team/junit/wiki/Categories`.

Populating suites automatically

Since the maintenance of suite classes and/or category annotations is often considered somewhat tedious, people have searched for ways to organize test runs automatically. The Eclipse IDE, for instance, provides the capability to run all JUnit tests determined by a project or package selection out of the box. However, this granularity doesn't match every need. Again, assume that you want to run each unit test on a regular basis that belongs to a specific subsystem. Furthermore, this time, the code might comprise more than one source project.

A popular solution is based on class name filters. The idea is to post or prefix class names of test cases with appropriate category names. Instead of `FooTest`, you could use `FooUnitTest`, `FooIntegrationTest`, `FooITest`, or whatever you prefer. The suite runner scans the classpath and selects only those test cases the fully qualified names of which match a regular expression. `ClasspathSuite`, *[CPSUIT]*, is a third-party runner that goes down that road:

```
@RunWith(ClasspathSuite.class)
@ClassnameFilters( {
  ".*Test",
  "!.*ITest"
} )
public class AllUnitTestCpSuite {}
```

This example reveals how class name filters are declared with the @ `ClassnameFilters` annotation. In our case, we run all tests with the postfix `Test`, but replace those with the postfix `ITest`. Of course, the regular expression approach allows us to filter out specific package names or the like. If you happen to work with integration tests related to OSGi, *[OSGIAL]*, a suite runner working accordingly is `BundleTestSuite`, *[OSGITE]*.

Admittedly, the use of naming conventions for categorization has some kind of smell to it because the collection of tests can easily be incomplete simply due to typos in a test case's name, which in turn could lead to unrecognized holes in our safety net. On the other hand, the name tells us "this is the integration test for the component `Foo`", or "this is the unit test for the component `Foo`", which makes it look a bit less bad. But certainly, it restricts test categorization to the class level.

How about creating test doubles with annotations?

Mockito provides a processor that generates and assigns test double fields implicitly. The following code snippet shows how we can use this approach in `TimelineTest`:

```
@RunWith( MockitoJUnitRunner.class )
public class TimelineTest {

  @Mock
  private SessionStorage storage;

  [...]
}
```

Unfortunately, there are a few imperfections, which one should bear in mind when using this solution. Recall *Chapter 2, Writing Well-structured Tests*, where we heard about the different fixture setup possibilities. In this context, we've mentioned as a downside of the implicit pattern that tests may lack readability. A similar concern is related to the @Mock annotation. It tempts the test case author to favor implicit test double creation, which again might be perfectly alright on small and simple structured classes. But it might blur coherence if applied to fields, which are hardly used in any test.

Yet more important is the fact that runners work exclusively. Their capabilities cannot be combined. If you, for example, need dataset tests, as introduced in the next section, you simply can't use the test double generator simultaneously. So, you would have to add an implicit initialization via MockitoAnnotations.initMocks or switch back to explicit stand-in creation. So, if you happen to advocate the @Mock approach, you might be better off anyway to facilitate this with the MockitoRule instead. Rules are explained in *Chapter 6, Reducing Boilerplate with JUnit Rules*.

Summarizing runners can have a pretty big *but* compared to the relatively small *value add* they provide. Hence, once more, the advice is not to overdo things. Always ensure that there is a reasonable advantage or necessity that justifies the use of a particular type.

Writing dataset tests

The last section of this chapter will cover one of the most important usage scenarios for runners. It'll explain the sense and purpose of tests that run against specific data records and presents the advantages and disadvantages of the available approaches.

Using parameterized tests

Given all this new and fancy knowledge about pluggable processors, it's about time to advance our TimelineTest. One of the main functionalities our component provides is the ability to fetch items page-wise. But there are quite a few preconditions that determine the behavior of item fetching. This leads to just as many tests, which barely differ in their structure. Instead of rewriting the same pattern over and over again, wouldn't it be nice to reuse a common test and simply provide behavior defining pre- and post-conditions as a set of data beans?

In fact, there is more than one canned solution based on runner extensions. Let's start with the built-in mechanism of JUnit, the `Parameterized` test processor. The basic idea is to define a collection of uniform object arrays, each of which represents a data record. Parameterized tests originally had to provide a public constructor with an argument list matching the field types of these arrays. Nowadays, it's possible to assign the parameters given by the records to dedicated fields automatically. The processor creates for every record and test combination a new test case instance injecting the data. Storing the data in fields of the test case enables us to use them as input and expected outcome throughout all tests.

Sounds complicated? Have a look at the modified `TimelineTest` version that comes next for a better understanding. Note how the annotation `@Parameters` marks `data`, the necessary data providing method. Parameter methods use the public and static modifiers and usually return a collection of object arrays. But if a test run needs a single parameter, we don't have to wrap it within an extra array and can return the parameter list as a simple object array, as shown next.

The actual data-supplying implementation delegates to a particular test helper type, a so-called data provider. Data providers are handy for reuse or to straighten up a test case. Stay tuned. We'll survey `FetchItemsDataProvider` in detail in just a minute.

We've already mentioned that we only expect a single parameter per test run, which is, in our case, an instance of the utility data type `FetchItemsData`. Note how the `@Parameter` annotation of the public field `data` facilitates the assignment of this parameter. Application of a structured data type can be helpful to avoid test cases bloated with too many fields. Having this in place, the `fetchItems` test can retrieve the input and expected outcome for the fixture setup and verification from the data bean:

```
@RunWith( Parameterized.class )
public class TimelineTest {

  @Parameter
  public FetchItemsData data;

  [...]

  @Parameters
  public static Object[] data() {
    return new Object[] {
      fetchItemsOnLowerFetchCountBound(),
      fetchItemsIfFetchCountExceedsItemCount()
    };
  }

  @Test
```

```
public void fetchItems() {
  itemProvider.addItems( data.getInput() );
  timeline.setFetchCount( data.getFetchCount() );
  timeline.fetchItems();

  timeline.fetchItems();
  List<Item> actual = timeline.getItems();

  assertArrayEquals( data.getOutput(),
                     actual.toArray() );
}

[...]
}
```

Every test method gets executed once for each sample specification supplied by the two data-providing methods of FetchItemsDataProvider. They are used by means of static imports for compactness. Of course, it's possible to use a single delegation method to finish off data provisioning in one go, but the different test scenarios would have fallen from view, which seemed a bit coarse-grained to begin with.

What remains is the FetchItemsData bean, which is pretty straight forward, using a fluent interface API for smooth initialization. Due to the book's line-length limitations, the item fields are simply denoted as input and output for brevity but could otherwise be more telling, such as expectedOutcome or the like:

```
public class FetchItemsData {

  private int fetchCount;
  private Item[] input;
  private Item[] output;

  public static FetchItemsData newFetchItemsData() {
    return new FetchItemsData();
  }

  public FetchItemsData withInput( Item ... input ) {
    this.input = input;
    return this;
  }

  public FetchItemsData withFetchCount( int fetchCount ) {
    this.fetchCount = fetchCount;
    return this;
  }
```

```java
  public FetchItemsData withOutput( Item ... output ) {
    this.output = output;
    return this;
  }

  public int getFetchCount() {
    return fetchCount;
  }

  public Item[] getInput() {
    return input;
  }

  public Item[] getOutput() {
    return output;
  }
}
```

At long last, let's examine the `FetchItemsDataProvider` class. It contains methods defining the input and expected outcome for certain test scenarios. Each scenario is represented by one method. Naturally, their amount is also restricted here for lack of space:

```java
public class FetchItemsDataProvider {

  private static final FakeItem FIRST_ITEM = new FakeItem( 10 );
  private static final FakeItem SECOND_ITEM = new FakeItem( 20 );
  private static final FakeItem THIRD_ITEM = new FakeItem( 30 );

  static FetchItemsData fetchItemsOnLowerFetchCountBound() {
    return FetchItemsData.newFetchItemsData()
      .withInput( FIRST_ITEM, SECOND_ITEM, THIRD_ITEM )
      .withFetchCount( Timeline.FETCH_COUNT_LOWER_BOUND )
      .withOutput( THIRD_ITEM, SECOND_ITEM );
  }

  static FetchItemsData fetchItemsIfFetchCountExceedsItemCount() {
    return FetchItemsData.newFetchItemsData()
      .withInput( FIRST_ITEM, SECOND_ITEM, THIRD_ITEM )
      .withFetchCount( 2 )
      .withOutput( THIRD_ITEM, SECOND_ITEM, FIRST_ITEM );
  }
}
```

Now, we are able to run our restructured test case. The following screenshot shows how the JUnit UI will depict the test results:

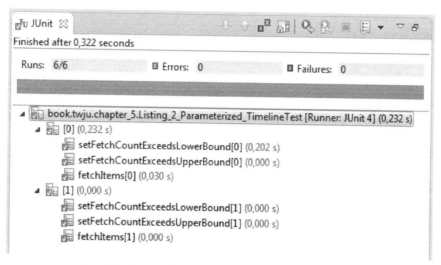

Result depiction of a test run with the Parameterized runner

We see that `fetchItems` truly gets executed twice. But wait a moment, every other nonparameterized test is also executed twice. This isn't very desirable as it falsifies the amount of actual useful test runs and unnecessarily increases the duration of execution. So, we have to either split `TimelineTest` or use another runner that claims to do better.

Reducing glue code with JUnitParams

To make a long story short, the library JUnitParams, *[JUNITP]*, offers a processor that allows us to attach data providers to specific test methods. This omits the glue code for the separate field allocation of the previous approach. Its incorporation into our example requires essentially only the moving of the `data` collecting method from `TimelineTest` to the data provider and renaming it to `provideData`, as shown in the next code snippet; this is because the runner expects data suppliers to start with the prefix `provide`:

```
public class FetchItemsDataProvider {

  private static final FakeItem FIRST_ITEM = new FakeItem( 10 );
  private static final FakeItem SECOND_ITEM = new FakeItem( 20 );
  private static final FakeItem THIRD_ITEM = new FakeItem( 30 );

  public static Object[] provideData() {
    return new Object[] {
```

```
        fetchItemsOnLowerFetchCountBound(),
        fetchItemsIfFetchCountExceedsItemCount()
    };
}

[...]

}
```

Next, we adjust our test case again. Most notably, `fetchItems` has an additional annotation, `@Parameters`, referring to our data-providing type. But on closer inspection, it occurs to us that the test method also expects a `FetchItemsData` instance as an argument:

```
@RunWith( JUnitParamsRunner.class )
public class TimelineTest {

    [...]

    @Test
    @Parameters( source = FetchItemsDataProvider.class )
    public void fetchItems( FetchItemsData data ) {
        itemProvider.addItems( data.getInput() );
        timeline.setFetchCount( data.getFetchCount() );
        timeline.fetchItems();

        timeline.fetchItems();
        List<Item> actual = timeline.getItems();

        assertArrayEquals( data.getOutput(),
                           actual.toArray() );
    }

    [...]
}
```

This solution appears to be slimmer, better readable, and more flexible than its precursor. The `@Parameters` annotation even facilitates various ways of data definition. Among others, the direct listing of string-encoded literals is supported. So, it seems as if we've struck gold. Let's behold the result depiction of the JUnit UI for this matter:

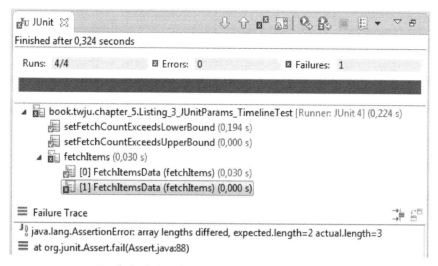

Result depiction of a test run with JunitParamsRunner

Indeed, this looks better. The `fetchItems` test is executed twice, while the nonparameterized tests are executed only once. The overall test method count is correct and no test execution time gets wasted. Eureka! Mission accomplished!

Well, almost. Examining the failing test in the preceding screenshot, we have difficulties in finding out which scenario actually does not work. Neither the test index nor the message gives us a human-understandable clue. Probably, we can improve this situation by equipping our data beans with more specific result messages. But before doing so, we prefer to check another approach based on datasets providing enum.

Increasing the expressiveness of test descriptions with Burst

The basic idea of Burst, *[BURST]*, turn out to be quite similar to JUnitParams, where data is mapped to specific test methods. But this time, data records are provided as elements of Java enum types. In doing so, the name of each element can be determined at runtime and supplied to the test's description. The next listing shows how we can convert `FetchItemsData` into such an enum:

```
public enum FetchItemsEnum {

  ON_LOWER_FETCH_COUNT_BOUND {
    @Override
    void init() {
      withInput( FIRST_ITEM, SECOND_ITEM, THIRD_ITEM );
```

```
                withFetchCount( Timeline.FETCH_COUNT_LOWER_BOUND );
                withOutput( THIRD_ITEM, SECOND_ITEM );
        }
    },

    ON_FETCH_COUNT_EXCEEDS_ITEM_COUNT {
        @Override
        void init() {
            withInput( FIRST_ITEM, SECOND_ITEM, THIRD_ITEM );
            withFetchCount( 2 );
            withOutput( THIRD_ITEM, SECOND_ITEM, FIRST_ITEM );
        }
    };

    private int fetchCount;
    private Item[] input;
    private Item[] output;

    FetchItemsEnum() {
        init();
    }

    abstract void init();

    [...]
}
```

We just introduced an abstract initialization method `init` to be able to configure each data element according to the scenarios provided by our data provider. The names for the elements might appear a bit unusual but add up to a fluent, readable test description as we'll see soon. Note that we've merged the data provider and data bean functionalities for brevity here, which requires the test item constants to be defined in a separate class (used with static imports). This is because they can't be initialized prior to the element's initialization if they are defined within the enum. Of course, it would also be possible to write a separate enum backed up by our existing data provider.

Finally, we have to adjust `TimelineTest` one last time:

```
@RunWith( BurstJUnit4.class )
public class TimelineTest {

    @Test
    public void fetchItems( FetchItemsEnum data ) {
        itemProvider.addItems( data.getInput() );
```

```
        timeline.setFetchCount( data.getFetchCount() );
        timeline.fetchItems();

        timeline.fetchItems();
        List<Item> actual = timeline.getItems();

        assertArrayEquals( data.getOutput(),
                           actual.toArray() );
    }


    [...]
    }
```

It's striking that `fetchItems` gets along without any additional annotation. The test is called for each element of the enum type. So, if a dataset can be packed easily into an enum, this solution appears to be not so bad either. But how does the UI result depiction look?

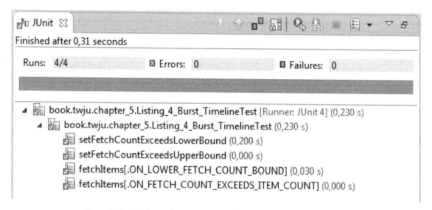

Result depiction of a test run with the BurstJUnit4 runner

The `fetchItems` test gets executed twice, while the non parameterized tests are executed only once. The overall test method count is correct, and no test execution time is wasted. Plus, this time, we've got more expressive hints about what a test run is all about.

 But bear in mind that Burst is still pretty new at the time of writing this, hence it might still have to prove its suitability for daily use.

In case you are wondering about the extra level in the result's tree structure, the tool allows additional constructor parameterization with enum. The second level is reserved to be able to depict the outcome of such runs. You may have also recognized the dot prior the enum element name. This is caused by the abstract type approach. Nonabstract types will be shown with the simple class name before the dot.

Once again, it's up to you to make a choice. But bear in mind that all presented solutions have a common tradeoff as input and outcome definitions are separated from the test phases. This makes them more difficult to read and impedes error tracking because failure traces do not point to a specific input/output combination perceptible from your code base. Thus, it can also be argued that parameterized tests be omitted for a manageable amount of preconditions. Before moving on to the next chapter, let's wrap up what we've learned about runners.

Summary

In this chapter, you acquired a thorough understanding of JUnit's runner architecture. You learned how to write your own extension and saw how it interacts with the tool's runtime. Based on this knowledge, we encountered several options to structure and categorize the entirety of our tests and discussed the downside of over-extensive runner use. We concluded the topic by explaining the assets and drawbacks of the different approaches to writing parameterized tests—one of the most important use cases for runners.

In the next chapter, you'll learn about a particular type of test helper that eases fixture setup and secures our tests with an automated teardown. We'll see how JUnit Rules embed tests at runtime and learn how to develop and use our own rules.

6
Reducing Boilerplate with JUnit Rules

We already explained how to minimize clutter and redundancy in test cases by extracting coherent utility code into separate test helpers, as seen in *Chapter 3, Developing Independently Testable Units*. In this chapter, you'll learn how to enhance this strategy by means of JUnit rules. You'll be given an introduction to the approach's mechanics and potential. To deepen this knowledge, we'll continue by writing and varying a sample extension. Then, we'll examine advanced features of rules-related functionality and conclude with the inspection of useful third-party vendor offerings. In short, this will make us capable of the following:

- Understanding rules
- Working with advanced concepts
- Employing custom solutions

Understanding rules

The benefits of JUnit rules, especially when dealing with integration tests, can hardly be overrated. That's why, we start with a thorough explanation of how they work and how you can implement your own extensions. This will put you in a position to increase your daily work efficiency with the aid of custom rules.

What are JUnit rules?

"Pedantry and mastery are opposite attitudes toward rules."

– George Pólya

JUnit offers a particular test helper support that we've already encountered in the course of this book. Recollect the introduction of the `ExpectedException` rule in *Chapter 4*, *Testing Exceptional Flow*, where you got a first impression of the possible applications. But what are rules exactly?

To answer this question, let's take a look at an example. Until now, we've concentrated our efforts on unit tests, which use DOCs as stand-in components to isolate SUTs from their dependencies. But at some point in time, you'll have to turn towards these dependencies, provide real-world implementations, and verify their correct behavior. This is when you write tests that incorporate costly system calls and third-party libraries and potentially span over several application layers—in short, integration tests.

As you've already learned, these are important flanking activities to separate our application code—the code we are in control of—from extrinsic influences. Unfortunately, this test type is considerably more expensive than a unit test because it has to deal with things such as environmental settings, framework startup, and last but not least, housekeeping.

Assume that we've decided to store our timeline state on the local filesystem. Hence, we'd need an appropriate `SessionStorage` realization. It seems natural to develop such `FileSessionStorage` against a proper integration test, but this involves dealing with tedious filesystem demands. First, there is the determination of a platform-independent storage location, and second, we have to clean up the remains after a test run.

Obviously, it's a pretty common challenge that cries out for a test helper. For this reason, JUnit provides the `TemporaryFolder` class. To avoid running into file access privilege trouble, it makes sense to choose storage locations for test output below the system's temporary directory. As the name implies, the helper offers several API methods for the creation of files or directories (below the temporary directory root) and a cleanup functionality, `delete`. The latter removes all content from the disk that has been originated by a temporary folder instance.

From what we've learned until now, we'd probably expect to use this helper as follows:

1. Create the storage location during test setup.
2. Call the `delete` method in an `@After` annotated method to do the housekeeping.

But since `TemporaryFolder` is a rule, the second step isn't necessary. The only thing we need to do is to register the rule correctly. Regard the `SessionStorage` interface and a simplistic `Memento` type sufficient for our considerations here. The storage reads and writes state mementos. The following code shows this:

```
public interface SessionStorage {
  void store( Memento memento );
  Memento read();
}
```

The state holder itself oversimplifies serialization a bit by employing a parameterized constructor and the `toString` method for this purpose. But this shouldn't bother us in the context of the current topic. We'll refine this approach in *Chapter 7, Improving Readability with Custom Assertions*. The following code shows this:

```
public class Memento {

  private String content;

  public Memento( String content ) {
    this.content = content;
  }

  @Override
  public String toString() {
    return content;
  }

  [...]
}
```

Let's apply our main attention to the following `FileSessionStorageITest` listing instead. As you can see, the temporary folder instance is created implicitly during field initialization. The `temporaryFolder` public field is annotated with `@Rule`. This is how rules have to be registered. But before we explain the reason for this, we'll complete the test case's examination first:

```
public class FileSessionStorageITest {

  private static final String CONTENT = "content";
```

```
@Rule
public TemporaryFolder temporaryFolder = new TemporaryFolder();

private FileSessionStorage storage;
private File storageLocation;

@Before
public void setUp() throws IOException {
  storageLocation = temporaryFolder.newFile();
  storage = new FileSessionStorage( storageLocation );
}

@Test
public void store() throws IOException {
  Memento memento = new Memento( CONTENT );

  storage.store( memento );

  assertEquals( CONTENT, readStoredContent() );
}

@Test
public void read() throws IOException {
  writeContentToStore( CONTENT );

  Memento memento = storage.read();

  assertEquals( CONTENT, memento.toString() );
}

[...]

private String readStoredContent() throws IOException {
  byte[] bytes = Files.readAllBytes( storageLocation.toPath() );
  return new String( bytes, StandardCharsets.UTF_8 );
}

private Path writeContentToStore( String content )
  throws IOException
{
  byte[] bytes = content.getBytes( StandardCharsets.UTF_8 );
  return Files.write( storageLocation.toPath(), bytes );
}
}
```

The basic idea is to use the file session storage to serialize a memento to a content string and store this on the local filesystem. Afterwards, we load the actual content from the file and check that it matches the expected one. For the verification of the read functionality, we proceed conversely. See how we rely always on the storage location provided by our test helper.

It is noteworthy that the store and read utility methods may indicate a code redundancy with respect to the component's implementation. We could get rid of this duplication using the storage itself to complete the particular turnarounds. Nevertheless, it seemed more plausible to have them here for initial understanding. Furthermore, we assume that the storage file already exists. Among other things, it would be worthwhile to verify how the storage deals with a situation where the file doesn't exist. So, feel free to refactor and complement the preceding listing appropriately as an exercise.

Now, it's about time to focus our attention on the rule mechanics. Rules provide a possibility of intercepting test method calls similar as an AOP framework would do. Comparable to an *around advice* in AspectJ, [ASPECT], the test method gets embedded dynamically into a code block. This allows the inserting of useful functionality before and/or after the actual test execution. It even enables you to skip the original call completely. Thus, the temporary folder instance is able to delete its files after a test run automatically.

But bear in mind that a test run in that regard includes the `@Before` and `@After` annotated callbacks because they constitute implicitly executed test phases. The rule clamp has to embrace these invocations, which in turn, explains why the rule's field initialization takes place at construction time. The rule simply has to exist before any testing-related action happens, to avoid interleaving. The tool creators probably found this manner sufficient and refrained from introducing, for example, another callback type.

While these abstract explanations surely sound reasonable, the best way to obtain a profound understanding is to write a rule by yourself. Although you might anticipate this to be complicated, it's actually a pretty simple thing to do.

Writing your own rule

The API part of a rule definition has to implement TestRule. The only method of this interface is apply, which returns an instance of Statement. Statement represents — simplistically spoken — your tests within the JUnit runtime and Statement#evaluate() executes them. Inspecting the argument list of apply, we recognize that a statement is also given as an input. The basic thought is to provide a wrapper extension of Statement, which can implement additional contributions by overriding evaluate:

```java
public class MyRule implements TestRule {

  @Override
  public Statement apply( Statement base,
                          Description description )
  {
    return new MyStatement( base );
  }
}

class MyStatement extends Statement {

  private final Statement base;

  MyStatement( Statement base ) {
    this.base = base;
  }

  @Override
  public void evaluate() throws Throwable {
    System.out.println( "before" );
    try {
      base.evaluate();
    } finally {
      System.out.println( "after" );
    }
  }
}
```

The preceding listing shows how a statement adapter works. Embedding the delegating evaluate call into a try-finally block ensures that, no matter what happens during the invocation, the console output 'before' and 'after' gets written. MyRuleTest confirms that our custom extension MyRule can be used in the same way as TemporaryFolder:

```java
public class MyRuleTest {

  @Rule
```

```
public MyRule myRule = new MyRule();

@Test
public void testRun() {
  System.out.println( "during" );
}
}
```

Launching the test case leads to the output depicted in the following image. This proves that our example rule works as expected. The test execution gets intercepted and modified by our rule to print `before` and `after` around the `during` of the test method.

MyRuleTest console output

Doing something before and after a test run is particularly typical for rules dealing with external resources, such as files, sockets, servers, database connections, and so on. So, it isn't surprising that there is a common super class for such use cases. The current example could be rewritten by extending `ExternalResource`, as indicated here:

```
public class MyRule extends ExternalResource {

  @Override
  protected void before() {
    System.out.println( "before" );
  }

  @Override
  protected void after() {
    System.out.println( "after" );
  }
}
```

Now that the very basics of rule development have been understood, we'll go a step further and cover a more advanced, yet very popular, pattern.

Configuring the fixture with annotations

Up to this point, we apply rules if we want to take care of a certain aspect that relates to all tests of a test case. Special fixture adjustments are done within each test method by calling the rule's helper methods. But sometimes, these configurations may not add much to the comprehension of the test's purpose or an aspect may not be related to all tests.

In these instances, it might be appropriate to combine a rule with an additional control annotation to reduce, for example, the clutter within a test. Remember the `@Mock` annotation mentioned in the preceding chapter? We've heard about the `MockitoRule` picking up marked fields and created test double instances on the fly—before the actual test execution started.

Later, on we'll encounter another useful application, but first, let's examine how we can evolve `MyRule` to enable test-specific settings by means of annotations. To do so, we introduce a method-related annotation, `MyRuleConfiguration`, which accepts a string value as a parameter:

```
@Retention(RetentionPolicy.RUNTIME)
@Target({ElementType.METHOD})
public @interface MyRuleConfiguration {
  String value() default "";
}
```

It's possible to access test method annotations by the `Description` argument, which we haven't used until now. This allows us to supplement the console output with the specified configuration value. The `MyConfigurableRule` variant here illustrates the details:

```
public class MyConfigurableRule implements TestRule {

  @Override
  public Statement apply( Statement base,
                          Description description )
  {
    return new MyConfigurableStatement( base, description );
  }
}

class MyConfigurableStatement extends Statement {

  private final Description description;
  private final Statement base;
```

```
MyConfigurableStatement( Statement base,
                        Description description )
{
    this.description = description;
    this.base = base;
}

@Override
public void evaluate() throws Throwable {
    String configuration = getConfiguration();
    System.out.println( "before [" + configuration + "]" );
    try {
        base.evaluate();
    } finally {
        System.out.println( "after [" + configuration + "]" );
    }
}

private String getConfiguration() {
    return description
        .getAnnotation( MyRuleConfiguration.class )
        .value();
}
}
```

This is all we have to do to bring MyRuleConfiguration into action. In the next snippet, MyConfigurableRuleTest shows its appropriate use:

 Note the additional annotation on the testRun method.

```
public class MyConfigurableRuleTest {

  @Rule
  public MyConfigurableRule myConfigurableRule
    = new MyConfigurableRule();

  @Test
  @MyRuleConfiguration( "myConfigurationValue" )
  public void testRun() {
    System.out.println( "during" );
  }
}
```

In the end, the console output will respect the configuration value, as displayed in the following image:

The MyRuleTest console output with annotation

Being able to write our own rules gives us a pretty good insight into how they are working. All the more, it's interesting to learn what some out-of-the-box implementations are capable of.

Working with advanced concepts

JUnit comes with a set of readymade rules, taking away some of the burden of common test-related development tasks, and we've already encountered a few of them. But the tool offers additional capabilities, allowing us to apply and combine rules in a way so as to meet special requirements, at which we'll have a look in the following section.

Using ClassRules

At times, integration tests need access to external resources, which can be expensive to establish. If these resources do not contribute more to the precondition of any test, rather than being an environmental invariant, testing individual creations and disposing of them might be a waste.

Think of an application server necessary as the infrastructure to provide the REST services you intend to validate. The application server does not contribute any test-specific state. It simply has to be there to be able to deploy, test, and undeploy REST resources on the fly. Because of this, it would be desirable to perform the following actions:

1. Start the server *once* before the service tests are executed.

2. Stop it as soon as these tests are done.

JUnit supports this with the aid of class rules. These are public, static fields of test cases annotated with `@ClassRule`. Eagerly created, they also have to be a subtype of `TestRule`. They can affect the operation of a whole test case, which means the execution of the *complete sequence* of its tests is embedded into a rule's `Statement#evaluate` call.

For better understanding, let's sketch the preceding application server use case. Consider `ServerRule`, which is responsible for starting and stopping a server instance. It would extend `ExternalResource` and may accept a port as a constructor argument. We do not really work with a server here but rather indicate the life cycle events with console output messages:

```java
public class ServerRule extends ExternalResource {

  private final int port;

  public ServerRule( int port ) {
    this.port = port;
  }

  @Override
  protected void before() throws Throwable {
    System.out.println( "start server on port: " + port );
  }

  @Override
  protected void after() {
    System.out.println( "stop server on port: " + port );
  }
}
```

Moreover, we provide `MyServerTest` to represent a set of tests that expects the server instance to be up and running. Again, we indicate this only with messages written to the console.

> Note how we use the `TestName` rule to determine the name of a test.

```java
public class MyServerTest {

  @Rule
  public TestName name = new TestName();

  @Test
```

```
    public void runFirstServerTest() {
      System.out.println( name.getMethodName() );
    }

    @Test
    public void runSecondServerTest() {
      System.out.println( name.getMethodName() );
    }
  }
```

Due to the fact that any subclass of `ParentRunner` will support class rules, it's feasible to aggregate all server-dependent test cases. `ServerIntegrationTestSuite` uses the `ClasspathSuite` runner introduced in *Chapter 5, Using Runners for Particular Testing Purposes*, to do so:

```
  @RunWith( ClasspathSuite.class )
  @ClassnameFilters( { ".*ServerTest" } )
  public class ServerIntegrationTestSuite {

    @ClassRule
    public static ServerRule serverRule = new ServerRule( 4711 );
  }
```

The suite will first "start" our server, then pick up any test cases prefixed with `ServerTest`, run all tests of these classes, and finally "stop" the server. The following screenshot of a test launch's output confirms the expected behavior:

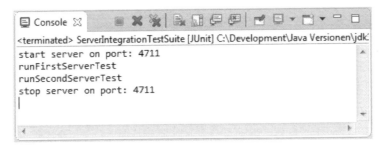

The MyServerTest console output

Although this approach has its advantages, there is a little downside too. Using class rules on suites, as explained previously, leads to a situation where a single test case loses its autonomy. It implies that running `MyServerTest` standalone isn't possible anymore. But you might have a lot of server-related test cases. Then, the overhead of starting and stopping the server for each of those separately might be too high, which, in turn, can justify this kind of suite solution.

The ordering of rule execution

Of course, it is feasible to employ more than one rule in a test case. In this instance, the rules' statement adapters get nested. However, in which sequence this will happen is undetermined. But sometimes, correct ordering is crucial. Consider, for example, a rule that depends on our server rule. It might deploy a service needed by all of the suite's aggregated tests. As a consequence, we would run into an error if the server isn't started first.

For such requirements, JUnit provides the `RuleChain` utility. Being an implementation of `TestRule`, it's registered just as any other rule. It allows you to compound rules in a way that defines their nesting order. The following listing enhances our server integration test suite to illustrate the usage:

```java
@RunWith( ClasspathSuite.class )
@ClassnameFilters( { ".*ServerTest" } )
public class ServerIntegrationTestSuite {

  @ClassRule
  public static TestRule chain = RuleChain
    .outerRule( new ServerRule( 4711 ) )
    .around( new MyRule() );
}
```

Rule chains are configured fluently. The `outerRule` static method marks the start of a chain, and each `around` call adds a nested rule instance. Running the suite and observing the console reveals how the `MyRule`-related messages are clamped within the `ServerRule` output but spans the succession of tests. The following screenshot shows this:

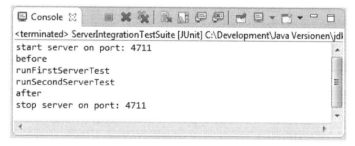

The MyServerTest console output with rule chaining

For a complete list and description of all built-in rules, please refer to the eponymic section of the JUnit documentation wiki at `https://github.com/junit-team/junit/wiki/Rules`.

Now, we'll continue with the introduction of useful little helpers provided by third-party vendors.

Employing custom solutions

Given the variety of possible applications, it's no wonder that there are custom rule solutions for both routine and fancy demands. Because of this, the last section of the chapter will dwell on noteworthy third-party implementations for each area.

Working with system settings

A source of constant burden is environment-specific functionality and state handling. Most of it is made accessible via the `java.lang.System` class. Setting and resetting system properties, capturing system output and so on produces quite a bit of overhead of boilerplate code. Luckily, a third-party utility called System Rules, *[SYSRUL]*, comes to the rescue. It encapsulates the redundancies and supplies several rules to accomplish the various tasks efficiently.

Let's have a quick look at some of the more common challenges and see how system rules will help. If you need to ensure that a particular system property is removed before test execution, you can use the `ClearSystemProperty` test helper. This rule deletes a property before a test run and restores the original value after a test run. The following example clears the predefined location of the temporary directory:

```
public class ClearPropertiesExample {

  private static final String JAVA_IO_TMPDIR = "java.io.tmpdir";

  @Rule
  public final ClearSystemProperties clearTempDirRule
    = new ClearSystemProperties( JAVA_IO_TMPDIR );

  @Test
  public void checkTempDir() {
    assertNull( System.getProperty( JAVA_IO_TMPDIR ) );
  }
}
```

Maybe more frequently, you want to define or override a particular system property for all tests. This can be achieved with the `ProvideSystemProperty` rule. Again, after a test run, the original value gets restored. The next example illustrates how you could alter (falsify) the value of the temporary directory property:

```
public class ProvideSystemPropertyExample {
```

```
private static final String JAVA_IO_TMPDIR = "java.io.tmpdir";
private static final String MY_TMPDIR = "/path/to/my/tmpdir";

@Rule
public final ProvideSystemProperty provideCustomTempDirRule
  = new ProvideSystemProperty( JAVA_IO_TMPDIR, MY_TMPDIR );

@Test
public void checkTempDir() {
  assertEquals( MY_TMPDIR,
              System.getProperty( JAVA_IO_TMPDIR ) );
}
}
```

But presumably, the most interesting is the `RestoreSystemProperties` helper. With this in place, you can simply set or change any property during a test. After a test run, the original values get restored. As this usage simply requires an appropriate rule definition, we omit any code snippets here.

Another common use case is that of capturing content that gets written to `System.out` or `System.err` print streams. For this purpose, the `SystemOutRule` and `SystemErrRule` rules are made available. They provide several modes configurable by the methods `enableLog`, `mute`, and `muteForSuccessfulTests`. The first one activates the capturing of content, the second prevents write through to the original stream. The last one does the same but allows messages to pass in the event of a test failure. The following snippet shows how to capture output but suppresses message depiction for successful tests:

```
public class CaptureSystemOutputExample {

  private static final String OUTPUT = "output";

  @Rule
  public final SystemOutRule systemOutRule
    = new SystemOutRule().enableLog().muteForSuccessfulTests();

  @Test
  public void captureSystemOutput() {
    System.out.print( OUTPUT );

    assertEquals( OUTPUT, systemOutRule.getLog() );
  }
}
```

The last system helper we'll examine here allows the provision of text input. This can be read from the System.in input stream during a test. The TextFromStandardInputStream rule gets created by the emptyStandardInputStream factory method, as shown in the next code. It provides several methods to supply the content that should be dispatched to the input stream. The example uses provideLines to this end:

```java
public class ProvideSystemInputExample {

    private static final String INPUT = "input";

    @Rule
    public final TextFromStandardInputStream systemInRule
        = TextFromStandardInputStream.emptyStandardInputStream();

    @Test
    public void stubInput() {
        systemInRule.provideLines( INPUT );

        assertEquals( INPUT, readLine( System.in ) );
    }

    private String readLine( InputStream inputstream ) {
        return new Scanner( inputstream ).nextLine();
    }
}
```

 For a complete list and profound description of all system rules, please refer to the library's documentation at http://stefanbirkner.github.io/system-rules/index.html.

We'll conclude this chapter with a utility that can come in handy when you run into trouble with platform-specific functionality for example.

Ignoring tests conditionally

JUnit offers the possibility to ignore single tests. To do so, you mark a test method additionally with @Ignore. Different than simply commenting or deleting @Test, runners will report the number of skipped tests and tag them appropriately within the UI result view. It's even feasible to record the reason why a test is being ignored using the annotation's optional string parameter.

But why should we wish to tear a hole in our safety net by ignoring a test? Well, basically we shouldn't. Nevertheless there are situations where we might opt for *temporarily* skipping certain tests. Think about nondeterministic tests for example, which fail only intermittently when running our complete suite of tests.

> *"The trouble with non-deterministic tests is that when they go red, you have no idea whether it's due to a bug, or just part of the non-deterministic behavior."*

> *"Initially people will look at the failure report and notice that the failures are in non-deterministic tests, but soon they'll lose the discipline to do that. Once that discipline is lost, then a failure in the healthy deterministic tests will get ignored too."*

> *– [FOWL11]*

Thus, it's better to deactivate these tests temporarily, just in case we are not able to fix the problem on the spot. Fowler describes strategies on how to put such tests into quarantine. A low-level approach might include marking them with `@Ignore`. The advantage compared to deleting the `@Test` annotation is that ignored tests are reported and, hence, pop up as reminders of future work items.

However, there can be reasons that call for a more fine-grained control of when to skip a test. Some time ago, while working on an SWT-based UI, we ran into a platform-related issue. It turned out that on non-Windows platforms asserting whether an SWT widget has got the input focus does not work with automated tests. But we thought that to have a test up and running on one platform is better than nothing. Hence, we decided to ignore the focus-related tests on non-Windows systems for the time being.

In JUnit, assumptions are the built-in means to skip tests that aren't meaningful. Assume statements throw `AssumptionViolatedException` if a given condition isn't met. The default runner marks a test with an unfulfilled assumption as skipped. Have a look at the following snippet that illustrates the principle:

```
public class AssumptionTest {

  @Test
  public void ignored() {
    Assume.assumeFalse( true );
    // statements below this line are skipped
  }

  @Test
  public void executed() {
    Assume.assumeTrue( true );
    // statements below this line are executed
  }
}
```

The following screenshot shows how a test run with a failed assumption gets depicted in the UI. You can see clearly how the test named `ignored` is marked as skipped:

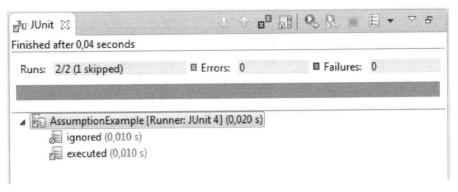

Test ignored with assume

But this approach tends to mingle test code with unrelated aspects. It seems more natural to separate the decision as to whether a test is to be ignored from the test's body. This is the notion behind `ConditionalIgnoreRule`, which uses the `@ConditionalIgnore` annotation to reach this goal, *[HERR13]*. `ConditionalIgnoreTest` demonstrates the concept as follows:

```
public class ConditionalIgnoreTest {

  @Rule
  public ConditionalIgnoreRule rule = new ConditionalIgnoreRule();

  @Test
  @ConditionalIgnore( condition = NotRunningOnWindows.class )
  public void focus() {
    // ...
  }
}

class NotRunningOnWindows implements IgnoreCondition {
  public boolean isSatisfied() {
    return
      !System.getProperty( "os.name" ).startsWith( "Windows" );
  }
}
```

@ConditionalIgnore requires a condition argument, pointing to a class that implements IgnoreCondition. IgnoreConditionRule picks up the annotation at runtime as described previously. It creates an instance of the condition-defining type and decides, based on the result of its isSatisfied method, whether a test should be skipped.

If so, AssumptionViolatedException is thrown. Therefore the ConditionalIgnore annotation has basically the same effect that an unmet Assume condition would have. It has the slight advantage that @Before and @After callbacks are also skipped.

Now that you know how to stick to the rules, let's shortly recap what you've learned in this chapter.

Summary

In this chapter, you acquired profound knowledge of the mechanics and capabilities of JUnit rules. You saw what it takes to write your own extension and learned how to evolve self-made rules by means of annotations. After that, you were imparted the usage of class rules on test suites and discussed the pros and cons of this approach. Besides, you were shown how rules can be nested in case your tests depend on a well-defined execution order. To round out the topic, we introduce third-party vendor solutions for common testing-related tasks.

The next chapter is devoted to the various available verification concepts. It will put the built-in assert functionality on a test and explain the assets and drawbacks of the most popular alternatives.

7
Improving Readability with Custom Assertions

In this chapter, you'll learn to write concise verifications that reveal the expected outcome of a test clearly. You'll be taught how domain-specific assertions help to improve readability and reduce boilerplate at the same time. To achieve this, you'll be given an overview of the respective capabilities and limitations of the various JUnit test verification techniques. In detail, you'll be introduced to the built-in mechanism, Hamcrest matchers, and AssertJ asserts. In this chapter, we will discuss the following topics:

- Working with the JUnit built-in assert approach
- Creating flexible expressions of intent with Hamcrest
- Writing fluently readable assertions with AssertJ

Working with the JUnit built-in assert approach

Starting with a short assertion definition recap, this section will give you an overview of JUnit's built-in verification mechanism. Advancing the example, we'll be confronted with more complex assertions and recognize how they impair readability. But we'll learn how to improve them by means of assertion test helpers. Finally, we'll discuss a few limitations of this approach.

Understanding the basics

By now, you comprehend why unit tests are usually arranged in phases. And it's clear that the outcome verification takes place in the third phase. The technical mechanism to achieve this is based on assertions. In principle, assertions check whether a Boolean predicate evaluates to true or false. In the event of the value false, an AssertionError is thrown. The runtime tool captures these errors and reports them as failures. As you already know, tests taking this approach are denoted as **self-checking**.

JUnit provides a built-in assertion utility, the class org.junit.Assert. It offers a couple of static convenient methods to ease validation. As they read better when referred by static imports, all listings in this book assume this implicitly. The following statements outline the essential variants:

```
fail();
fail( "Houston, we've got a problem." );

assertNull( identifier );
assertNull( "Identifier must not be null.",
            identifier );

assertTrue( counter.hasNext() );
assertTrue( "Counter should have a successor.",
            counter.hasNext() );

assertEquals( expected, actual );
assertEquals( "Expected value does not match actual.",
              expected,
              actual );
```

Let's continue with a closer look at each of these assertion methods:

- fail() throws an assertion error unconditionally. This might be helpful to mark an incomplete test (work in progress) or to ensure that an expected exception has been thrown (see *Chapter 4, Testing Exceptional Flow*).

- assertNull(Object) and assertNotNull(Object) are used to verify the initialization state of a variable. The first one asserts that the given argument is unassigned and the second one ensures that it is assigned.

- The assertTrue(boolean) and assertFalse(boolean) methods check the evaluation result of a Boolean expression. The invocation of the first method assumes the findings to be true, whereas the second method anticipates the opposite.

- `assertEquals(Object,Object)`, `assertNotEquals(Object,Object)`, `assertSame(Object,Object)`, and so on, and their equivalents for primitive types, are used for comparison verification of values, objects, and arrays. Although it makes no difference with respect to a test's outcome, it's important to pass the expected value as the first parameter and the actual as the second parameter. This is because it ensures the meaningfulness of failure messages.

All these methods provide overloaded versions that take an additional string parameter. In the event of a failure, the argument gets incorporated into the assertion error's message. Many people consider this helpful to express deficiencies more clearly. Others perceive such messages as clutter, making tests harder to read and more expensive to maintain. Throughout this book, we usually omit messages for the reason of brevity.

 For more information on specific assertion methods please refer to the JavaDoc utilities, *[ASSJAD]*.

Reviewing the file session storage

Before examining assert statements in practice and going ahead with our timeline example, we've first got to review the simple file session storage version from *Chapter 6, Reducing Boilerplate with JUnit Rules*. We've already noted that abusing a memento for persistence purposes probably isn't the best design choice. That's because the pattern is meant to capture and restore the internal state of a component without breaking encapsulation, *[GHJV96]*. It should not be made accountable for handling serialization by itself. This would imply more than one reason for the class to change and, hence, break the single responsibility principle (see *Chapter 3, Developing Independently Testable Units*).

Admittedly, we have to recall that `Item` is intended to have various implementations. This is because the presentation of a particular timeline instance depends, to some degree, on the characteristics of a concrete item type. And certainly, we need several collaborators, such as an appropriate item provider and a UI item factory, for successful adaption, but basically *extension and adaption requirements* are focused on the item's peculiarities.

However, our present approach exposes the memento to changes with respect to the different item types we may employ. But its functionality should be item type unrelated, and there should be no need to *modify* it. An insight that is compliant with the open/closed principle states:

> "*Software entities (classes, modules, functions, etc.) should be open for extension, but closed for modification.*"

– [OPECLO]

Reflecting this, we reduce `Memento` to be a plain-structured data type again. A simple version is shown in the next listing. It assumes that the state is defined by a set of items loaded by the timeline instance and a top item, which represents the upmost item scrolled into view. For compactness, we ignore any input validations or the like:

```java
public class Memento {

    private final Set<? extends Item> items;
    private final Item topItem;

    public Memento( Set<? extends Item> items, Item topItem ) {
        this.items = items;
        this.topItem = topItem;
    }

    public Set<? extends Item> getItems() {
        return items;
    }

    public Item getTopItem() {
        return topItem;
    }
}
```

The problem is that now we have to alter the storage implementations accordingly. And how shall we do the serialization anyway?

The example makes it obvious that the *test first* approach does not prevent us from making design decision mistakes. As always, when evolving a system, the lessons learned can call for substantial changes in the existing code. But having our safety net, we can determine exactly which specifications have to be adjusted. So, don't panic and *first* adapt the affected tests. *Second*, fix the SUTs. Once the bar is green again and the refactoring is done, you can be sure that the modified functionality has been introduced without breaking anything else. Everything will fall into place.

Applied to our example, we recognize that serialization apparently depends on a particular item's type. Thus, we introduce a new `ItemSerialization` interface—a collaborator used by our file item storage:

```
public interface ItemSerialization {
  String serialize( Item item );
  Item deserialize( String input );
}
```

The idea is to supply an individual implementation for each item type. The following listing shows the plain serialization of `FakeItem` appropriate for testing purposes:

```
public class FakeItemSerialization implements ItemSerialization {

  @Override
  public String serialize( Item item ) {
    return String.valueOf( item.getTimeStamp() );
  }

  @Override
  public Item deserialize( String input ) {
    return new FakeItem( parseLong( input ) );
  }
}
```

For completeness, we anticipate a little static helper, `FakeItems`, that provides test item definitions and the like to keep the subsequent version of `FileSessionStorageITest` more concise:

```
public class FakeItems {

  public static final FakeItem FIRST_ITEM = new FakeItem( 10 );
  public static final FakeItem SECOND_ITEM = new FakeItem( 20 );
  public static final FakeItem THIRD_ITEM = new FakeItem( 30 );

  public static final Set<FakeItem> ALL_ITEMS
     = unmodifiableSet(
        new HashSet<FakeItem>(
          asList( FIRST_ITEM, SECOND_ITEM, THIRD_ITEM ) ) );
}
```

Now it's about time we put things together.

Verifying the storage behavior

With all these preliminary considerations, we're ready to forge a bridge back and merge with the assert topic. If we look at the reworked storage test implementation that follows, we see that the fixture setup includes the new collaborator for item serialization. We pick up the thoughts from the preceding chapter and test the storage functionality in a single store-and-read cycle. The check verifies that the restored memento matches the initial one and asserts that, indeed, something gets written to the storage location.

As you can see, we are not interested any longer in the storage content or format, which is actually an internal detail of the storage class. The less we depend on internals, the better it is since we minimize the risk of breaking our test by refactoring the SUT:

```java
public class FileSessionStorageITest {

  @Rule
  public TemporaryFolder temporaryFolder = new TemporaryFolder();

  private ItemSerialization itemSerialization;
  private FileSessionStorage storage;
  private File storageLocation;

  @Before
  public void setUp() throws IOException {
    storageLocation = temporaryFolder.newFile();
    itemSerialization = new FakeItemSerialization();
    storage =
      new FileSessionStorage( storageLocation, itemSerialization );
  }

  @Test
  public void storage() throws IOException {
    Memento expected = new Memento( ALL_ITEMS, FIRST_ITEM );

    storage.store( expected );
    Memento actual = storage.read();

    assertEquals( expected.getTopItem(),
                  actual.getTopItem() );
    assertEquals( expected.getItems(),
                  actual.getItems() );
    assertNotSame( expected, actual );
```

```
      assertTrue( storedMemento().length > 0 );
  }

  private byte[] storedMemento() throws IOException {
    return Files.readAllBytes( storageLocation.toPath() );
  }
}
```

While all this seems reasonable, we're struggling a bit with the readability of the assert statements. This is why we'll inspect them in more detail in the next paragraph.

Improving readability with assertion helpers

To begin with, `assertEquals(Object,Object)` is backed up in essence by `Object.equals(Object)`. This means our first assertion can only work if `Item` derivatives are implementing the contract of `equals` and `hashCode`. Otherwise, we would have to check each item attribute separately. So, for brevity, let's assume this requirement has been realized by our `FakeItem` class.

However, not every data type may supply appropriate `equals` and `hashCode` methods. Well, `Memento` doesn't and — to build up the case — assume that we're not in a position to change it. This is when we'd have to swallow the pill and use more than one statement to verify the memento's equality. Aside from that, there are plenty of reasons for assertion conditions to get bulky, and in such cases, we may decide to extract coherent statements into intention-revealing helping-methods. We do this by providing expressive method names with respect to the underlying concept that the assertions are verifying.

But the more statements and helping methods are needed, usually the less readable and manageable the test case gets. Even in our simple example, it isn't recognizable at a glance; the memento-related outcome simply expects the initial state holder to be equal and not the same as the restored one. At this point, it's advisable to extract an assertion helper class — all the more if you have to write checks against a certain domain type in more than one test:

```
public class MementoAssert {

  public static void assertEqualsButNotSame( Memento expected,
                                             Memento actual )
  {
    assertTopItemEquals( expected, actual );
    assertItemsEquals( expected, actual );
    assertNotSame( "Mementos must not be the same.",
```

```
                      expected,
                      actual );
   }

   public static void assertItemsEquals( Memento expected,
                                          Memento actual )
   {
     Assert.assertEquals( "Memento items do not match\n",
       expected.getItems(),
         actual.getItems() );
   }

   public static void assertTopItemEquals( Memento expected,
                                           Memento actual )
   {
     Assert.assertEquals( "Memento top item does not match\n",
                          expected.getTopItem(),
                          actual.getTopItem() );
   }
 }
```

MementoAssert exemplarily provides several methods that are tailored for memento-related verifications. The functionality is actually backed up by JUnit's Assert type and uses several messages to clarify failure reasons. The next version of our storage test applies assertEqualsButNotSame(Memento,Memento) referred by static import and increases the intelligibility of the test's expected outcome:

```
public class FileSessionStorageITest {

  [...]

  @Test
  public void storage() throws IOException {
    Memento expected = new Memento( ALL_ITEMS, FIRST_ITEM );

    storage.store( expected );
    Memento actual = storage.read();

    assertEqualsButNotSame( expected, actual );
    assertTrue( storedMemento().length > 0 );
  }

  [...]
}
```

All that remains is to watch our assertion helper in action. The following image shows how trouble due to different top items would be displayed. To facilitate readability as depicted, Item derivatives, of course, have to supply recognizable toString implementations. The trace denotes a meaningful reason and ties in with the compared objects. But note that depending on our helper implementation, this might not be the only problem. We wouldn't know whether the mementos' item sets also differ. This is because the first failure shadows the second. But this constraint only has so much practical impact as the latter gets unveiled soon enough most of the time.

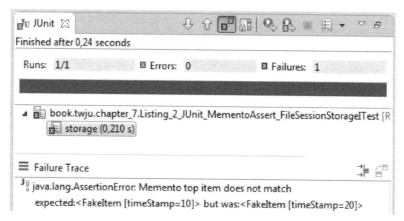

Failure message of MementoAssert

The JUnit assertion approach seems to be intuitive at first sight, which is why we used it in the previous chapters to get started. Besides, it's still quite popular and the tools support failure reporting well.

But looking at it more closely, it becomes clear that it's a bit limited and often makes it difficult to express conditions in a readable manner. Assume that you want to check a subset of attributes of a specific result type. You either have to write a single assertion statement for each of the attributes or retreat to a single assertTrue or assertFalse statement delegating the condition evaluation to a helper method. While this might be readable, it's hardly reusable for a slightly different set of attributes. Even if we write assertion helpers as shown earlier, we lack the advantages of an object-oriented approach. The latter would allow us to inherit and/or combine common verification functionality.

That's why there are alternative assertion strategies for self-checking tests. One is provided by the Hamcrest library, and the next section will explain how to use it with respect to our storage test.

Creating flexible expressions of intent with Hamcrest

The following paragraphs will introduce the essentials of how to apply Hamcrest matchers to test assertion and show you how to write your own predicate extensions.

Using matcher expressions

Hamcrest, *[HAMJAV]*, aims to provide an API to *create flexible expressions of intent*. The utility offers nestable predicates called `Matcher`s to do so. These allow writing complex verification conditions in a way which many developers consider easier to read than Boolean operator expressions.

Test assertion is supported by the `MatcherAssert` class. It offers the `assertThat(T, Matcher<? super T>)` static helper method. The first argument passed is the object to verify. The second is an appropriate predicate used to evaluate the first one:

```
assertThat( item.getTimeStamp(), equalTo( 10L ) );
```

Matcher implementations provide static factory methods for instantiation (above `IsEqual.equalTo(T)`). The intention is to mimic the flow of a natural language. This is made even more clear by the following statement. It uses `Is.is(Matcher<T>)` to decorate the original expression. The `Is` class is a `Matcher` subtype referred to as *syntactical sugar*. It retains the evaluation results of inner predicates and exists only for readability aspects:

```
assertThat( item.getTimeStamp(), is( equalTo( 10L ) ) );
```

Lookups of matcher factory methods are eased by the `org.hamcrest.CoreMatchers` helper class that subsumes the out-of-the-box predicates. Of course, there is also a matcher for negation:

```
assertThat( item.getTimeStamp(),
            is( not( equalTo( 20L ) ) ) );
```

`MatcherAssert.assertThat(...)` exists with two more signatures. First, there is a variant that takes a string and a Boolean parameter instead of the matcher argument. Its behavior correlates to `Assert.assertTrue(String, boolean)`. The second variant takes an additional string compared to the already known one. This can be used to improve the expressiveness of failure messages:

```
assertThat( "Item timestamp does not match expected values",
            item,
            either( equalTo( 10L ) ).or( equalTo( 20L ) ) );
```

As a side note, regard how the preceding statement combines two expressions logically with or.

Soon, we'll also see a variant for and. With this short introduction, let's try to rewrite the verifications of FileSessionStorageITest using Hamcrest expressions:

```java
public class FileSessionStorageITest {

  [...]

  @Test
  public void storage() throws IOException {
    Memento expected = new Memento( ALL_ITEMS, FIRST_ITEM );

    storage.store( expected );
    Memento actual = storage.read();

    assertThat( actual.getItems(),
                is( equalTo( expected.getItems() ) ) );
    assertThat( actual.getTopItem(),
                is( equalTo( expected.getTopItem() ) ) );
    assertThat( actual, is( not( sameInstance( expected ) ) ) );
    assertThat( "Memento has not been written to disk.",
                storedMemento().length > 0 );
  }

  [...]
}
```

Due to the simple nature of the example in this case, the advantages are moderate, but it should be sufficient to get an idea of the concept. The next subsection will demonstrate how to combine matchers in a bit more complex expression. As mentioned previously, the assertThat variant, which checks against a Boolean value, does not go without reason. Hence, the string parameter, when verifying the memento, actually gets written to the disk.

As already mentioned, the library comes with a set of useful matcher implementations. The most important ones are listed in the *Tour of common matchers* section of the library's online documentation. But for domain-specific problems, you can write your own extensions.

Writing custom matchers

The common base class for self-made matchers is `TypeSaveMatcher<T>`. It handles `null` checks and type safety. The generic parameter type `T` refers to the domain type the predicate is written for. In terms of our example, the `MementoMatcher` in the code following this information box shows an appropriate extension:

 Note how the factory method `equalTo(Memento)` gets annotated with `@Factory`, which is meant for tool support.

```java
public class MementoMatcher extends TypeSafeMatcher<Memento> {

  private Memento expected;

  @Factory
  public static Matcher<Memento> equalTo( Memento expected ) {
    return new MementoMatcher( expected );
  }

  @Override
  protected boolean matchesSafely( Memento actual ) {
    return actual.getItems().equals( expected.getItems() )
      && actual.getTopItem().equals( expected.getTopItem() );
  }

  @Override
  public void describeTo( Description description ) {
    String pattern = "\n  topItem: %s\n  items: %s";
    description.appendText( format( expected, pattern ) );
  }

  @Override
  protected void describeMismatchSafely( Memento actual,
                                         Description description )
  {
    String pattern = "\n    was:\n  topItem: %s\n  items: %s";
    description.appendText( format( actual, pattern ) );
  }

  private MementoMatcher( Memento expected ) {
    this.expected = expected;
  }
```

```
private static String format( Memento memento,
                                String pattern )
{
  return String.format( pattern,
                        memento.getTopItem(),
                        memento.getItems() );
}
}
```

The factual evaluation takes place in the `matchesSafely` method and checks memento attributes of both the expected and actual instances for equality. The given `actual` argument is the dispatched parameter of the `assertThat` statement of `MatcherAssert`. The `describeTo` and `describeMismatchSafely` methods are available to equip failure messages with a suitable breakdown of the expected and actual values. Different than the helper of the previous section, this time, all attributes are listed. The next excerpt rewrites the `storage` test, this time backed by the custom matcher. See how we are able to combine existing matchers with the new one:

```
public class FileSessionStorageITest {

  [...]

  @Test
  public void storage() throws IOException {
    Memento expected = new Memento( ALL_ITEMS, FIRST_ITEM );

    storage.store( expected );
    Memento actual = storage.read();

    assertThat( "Memento has not been written to disk.",
                storedMemento().length > 0 );
    assertThat( actual,
           is( both(
              equalTo( expected ) )
                .and( not(
                  sameInstance( expected ) ) ) ) );
  }

  [...]
}
```

Of course, it's also possible to write a matcher that checks `equalToButNotSame` in a single statement. But on one hand, we wanted to underline the combinability of custom and pre-built predicates, and on the other hand, this constitutes a good exercise for you to do it by yourself. Furthermore, please note the preceding example has been chosen to explain how to build up a matcher from the bottom. But there is also an easier way to achieve an `equalTo` functionality with respect to our `Memento` type. To do so, you can use the composition capability of the `AllOf` core matcher and the `HasPropertyWithValue` matcher provided by the `org.hamcrest.beans` package, as shown in the next snippet:

```
public static Matcher<Memento> equalTo( Memento expected ) {
   return allOf(
      hasProperty( "items",
        CoreMatchers.equalTo( expected.getItems() ) ),
      hasProperty( "topItem",
        CoreMatchers.equalTo( expected.getTopItem() ) ) );
}
```

Now, let's take a look at the following screenshot, which shows how a failing test result would look. Read through the detailed message. Although an assertion error gets raised by the first mismatch, this time, you can recognize all potential matcher-related problems at once. Nevertheless, if there are many attributes, the complete listing might tend to be a bit confusing because one can easily miss the woods for the trees.

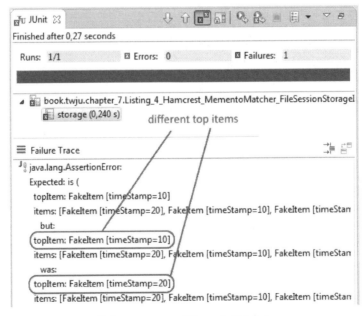

Failure message of MementoMatcher

It's a little unfortunate that JUnit expands the API of its Assert class to provide a set of assertThat (...) methods. These methods actually duplicate the API provided by MatcherAssert. In fact, the implementation of those methods delegates to the respective methods of this type.

Although this might look like a minor issue, I think it is worth a mention. Due to this approach, JUnit is firmly tied to the Hamcrest library. This dependency leads to problems every now and then; in particular, when used with other libraries, which do even worse by incorporating their own copy of a downgraded Hamcrest version.

But for the sake of completeness, it must be said that the JUnit developers are aware of these problems and intend to get independent from Hamcrest in the future.

Unit test assertions à la Hamcrest are not without competition. The library's verification statements are sometimes perceived as too verbose, and finding the correct factories while creating expressions can be a bit of a hurdle without special tool support. So, if you happen to be new to the library, you may wonder which expression to use and typing may feel a little uncomfortable. Because of this, let's have a look how AssertJ addresses the task of verification.

Writing fluently readable assertions with AssertJ

The last section of this chapter will explain the fundamentals of AssertJ and explain how to improve verification readability with custom extensions.

Employing assertion chains

In *Chapter 4*, *Testing Exceptional Flow*, one of the examples uses three assertXXX statements to check whether:

- An expected exception is not null
- It's an instance of IllegalArgumentException
- It provides a specific error message

The passage looks similar to the following snippet:

```
Throwable actual = ...

assertNotNull( actual );
assertTrue( actual instanceof IllegalArgumentException );
assertEquals( EXPECTED_ERROR_MESSAGE, actual.getMessage() );
```

Indeed, it takes a second or two to grasp the verification conditions. This is because there is a lot of redundant clutter: the relevant attributes of the `Throwable` type are checked one by one, always repeating the "assert" prefix and dispatching the `actual` parameter to the assertion statements. AssertJ, *[ASSERJ]*, strives to improve this by providing **fluent assertions for Java**. The intention behind the fluent interface API is to supply an easy-to-read, expressive programming style that reduces boilerplate and simplifies typing. So, this is how this approach can be used to refactor the foregoing code:

```
import static org.assertj.core.api.Assertions.assertThat;
```

Similar to the other approaches, this library provides a utility class that offers a set of static helper methods. Large sections of them are named `assertThat` and serve as overloaded factories, all returning extensions of `AbstractAssert`. The returned derivative depends on the particular type of the given argument and defines the validation possibilities available for the latter. This is the starting point for the so-called *statement chaining*.

```
Throwable actual = ...

assertThat( actual )
  .isInstanceOf( IllegalArgumentException.class )
  .hasMessage( EXPECTED_ERROR_MESSAGE );
```

The example returns an instance of `ThrowableAssert`, thus encapsulating the actual `Throwable` argument to check. Each verification method, in turn, gives back this very instance to enable the chaining mechanism.

 Note that we've omitted the `null` check here. This is because it's included as an explicit check by all verification methods ensuring a clear failure message.

While readability is, to some extent, in the eye of the beholder, at any rate, AssertJ assertions are very compact. See how the various verification aspects relevant for the specific concept under test are added fluently. This makes typing very efficient since the IDE's content assist can display a list of the available possibilities for a given value type automatically.

Do you want to provide expressive failure messages to the afterworld? One possibility is to use `describedAs` as the first link in the chain to comment the whole block:

```
String description
  = "Expected exception does not match specification.";

Throwable actual = ...

assertThat( actual )
  .describedAs( description )
  .hasMessage( EXPECTED_ERROR_MESSAGE )
  .isInstanceOf( NullPointerException.class );
```

The snippet expects `NullPointerException` but assumes that `IllegalArgumentException` is thrown at runtime. The failing test run would produce the message shown by the following screenshot:

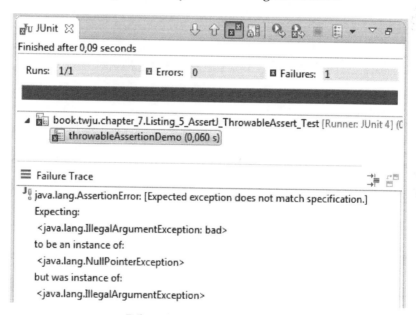

Failure message of ThrowableAssert

Perhaps you want your message to be more nuanced. In this case, you may add a `describedAs` statement before each verification method call:

```
Throwable actual = ...

assertThat( actual )
```

```
        .describedAs( "Message does not match specification." )
        .hasMessage( EXPECTED_ERROR_MESSAGE )
        .describedAs( "Exception type does not match specification." )
        .isInstanceOf( NullPointerException.class );
```

There are many more AssertJ capabilities to explore, especially the versatile assertion possibilities of collections, which are worth mentioning.

 But to keep this chapter in scope, please refer to the utility's online documentation for detailed information, *[ASSERJ]*.

Instead, we continue by rewriting our `storage` test once again:

```
public class FileSessionStorageITest {

    [...]

    @Test
    public void storage() throws IOException {
      Memento expected = new Memento( ALL_ITEMS, FIRST_ITEM );

      storage.store( expected );
      Memento actual = storage.read();

      assertThat( actual.getItems() )
        .isEqualTo( expected.getItems() );
      assertThat( actual.getTopItem() )
        .isEqualTo( expected.getTopItem() );
      assertThat( actual ).isNotSameAs( expected );
      assertThat( storedMemento() ).isNotEmpty();
    }

    [...]
}
```

Here, too, the advantages seem to be moderate at first glance. But looking at the storage check, the readability improves quite a bit due to the `AbstractByteArrayAssert` type. The assertion can be read like a natural language, and the meaning is clear at once. There is no need for our in-brain parser to evaluate any low-level Boolean expressions.

Well, before bringing this chapter to an end, we still have to explain how to write and apply custom assert types with AssertJ.

Creating your own asserts

Custom assertion helpers extend AbstractAssert, as shown in the next code snippet. The type's first generic parameter is the assert type itself. This is needed for the fluent chaining style. The second one defines the type based on which the assertion operates. MementoAssert overrides isEqualTo by delegating to two additional exemplary verification methods. These could be used in chaining expressions for partial equality checks. Because of this, they return the assert instance itself. The code snippet following this information box shows this:

> Note how calling isNotNull() ensures that the instance of Memento, which we want to check, can never be null.

```
public class MementoAssert
   extends AbstractAssert<MementoAssert, Memento>
{

   private static final String ITEM_PATTERN
     = "\nExpected items to be\n  <%s>,\nbut were\n  <%s>.";
   private static final String TOP_ITEM_PATTERN
     = "\nExpected top item to be\n  <%s>,\nbut was\n  <%s>.";

   public static MementoAssert assertThat( Memento actual ) {
     return new MementoAssert( actual );
   }

   public MementoAssert( Memento actual ) {
     super( actual, MementoAssert.class );
   }

   @Override
   public MementoAssert isEqualTo( Object expected ) {
     hasEqualItems( ( Memento )expected );
     hasEqualTopItem( ( Memento )expected );
     return this;
   }

   public MementoAssert hasEqualItems( Memento expected ) {
     isNotNull();
     if( !actual.getItems().equals( expected.getItems() ) ) {
       failWithMessage( ITEM_PATTERN,
                        expected.getItems(),
                        actual.getItems() );
```

```
      }
      return this;
    }

    public MementoAssert hasEqualTopItem( Memento expected ) {
      isNotNull();
      if( !actual.getTopItem().equals( expected.getTopItem() ) ) {
        failWithMessage( TOP_ITEM_PATTERN,
                         expected.getTopItem(),
                         actual.getTopItem() );
      }
      return this;
    }
  }
```

Note the `failWithMessage` call, which does the failure reporting. The given arguments are dispatched to `String.format` and, thereby, get incorporated into the assertion error's message. `MementoAssert` is intended to be created by its `assertThat(Memento)` factory method. Since it inherits the available base checks, the subclass can be used for more complex checks out of the box (see the following snippet):

```
assertThat( actual )
  .isNotSameAs( expected )
  .hasEqualItems( expected );
```

Last but not least, here comes the final version of `FileSessionStorageITest`, which uses `MementoAssert` for the equality check:

```
public class FileSessionStorageITest {

  [...]

  @Test
  public void storage() throws IOException {
    Memento expected = new Memento( ALL_ITEMS, FIRST_ITEM );

    storage.store( expected );
    Memento actual = storage.read();

    assertThat( storedMemento() ).isNotEmpty();
    assertThat( actual )
      .isEqualTo( expected )
      .isNotSameAs( expected );
  }

  [...]
}
```

The following screenshot shows how non-equal top-item instances leads to a failure and how this problem gets displayed:

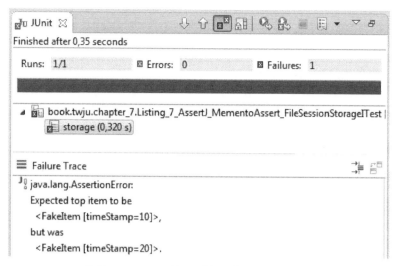

Failure message of AssertJ-based MementoAssert

A minor risk with the method chaining approach exists when writing a line of code, such as `assertThat(actual);`, meaning without any assertion calls. It would compile, but it wouldn't do anything useful. If `actual` is a Boolean object, a developer could assume, by mistake, that the code asserting the object is equal to `true`. Following the TDD practice of always starting with a failing test eliminates this risk, though, *[UTAS14]*.

Another problem with the fluent API approach is that single-line chained statements can be more difficult to debug. That is because debuggers are not able to set different breakpoints within a line. Likewise, it can be unclear which of the method calls may have caused an exception or failure.

But these issues can be overcome by breaking chained statements into multiple lines, as shown in the foregoing examples. This way, the user can set breakpoints within the chain and easily step through the code line by line.

As usual, after going through the references, we close the chapter with a summary of what we've have learned:

Summary

In this chapter, you were given an overview of the capabilities and limitations of the various JUnit test verification techniques. More precisely, you were introduced to the built-in mechanism, Hamcrest matchers, and AssertJ asserts. You learned about the difficulties involved in writing concise verifications to reveal the expected outcome of a test clearly. However, we experienced how domain-specific assertions can help to improve readability and reduce boilerplate at the same time.

In the upcoming, final chapter, we will wrap up the example application and conclude the book with a short introduction to continuous integration. The latter can be seen as the perfect JUnit testing complement to maintain short feedback cycles and provide quality-related reports for your whole team.

8
Running Tests Automatically within a CI Build

This last chapter will conclude the sample application and consider important test-related architectural aspects with respect to modularization. You'll learn how continuous integration superbly supplements the *test first* approach and increases the artifact delivery rate. For practice, we'll set up a timeline CI build based on Maven and finish with the incorporation of coverage reports. In this chapter, we will cover the following topics:

- Wrapping up the sample application
- Setting up an automated build
- Integrating code coverage reports

Wrapping up the sample application

In this section, we'll review some weak design spots of the example application and talk about the testing-related effects of higher-level concepts, such as modularization.

Refining the architecture

"To finish first you must first finish."

– Rick Mears

Throughout the previous chapters, you received an impression of how architectural fine-tuning goes hand in hand with the *test first* approach. You've experienced that a safety net of well-written tests prevents collateral damage on changes even if more substantial alterations due to the lessons learned in the course of system development should be necessary.

As a consequence, justified changes are less risky to achieve and, chances are, they get incorporated properly and consistently. This, in turn, promotes a healthy structure, freed of dull workarounds that bite back at any given opportunity. Obviously, software implemented that way is easier to maintain and faster to evolve. Overall, it improves the odds of meeting reasonable goals in time and within budget.

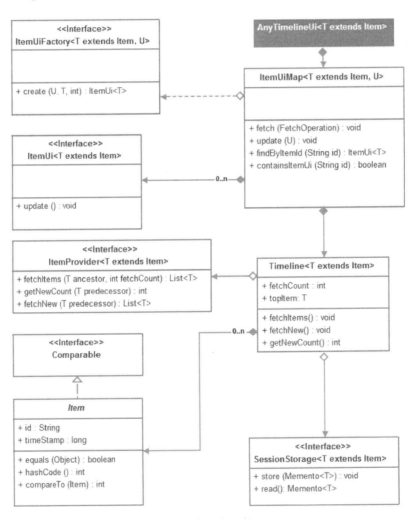

Refined timeline class diagram

As a matter of fact, writing tests first often reveals design flaws before they leave the developer's custody. Pointed corner case scenarios can very well clarify a component's insufficiency due to inappropriate interface definitions or the like. In this sense, let's fastforward our sample and see how our coarse-grained class structure of the beginning unfolds over time (see the preceding image).

The most evident changes introduce generic type parameters to a lot of the timeline classes. This ensures implicitly the use of collaborators with matching `Item` types. Admittedly, this is less an insight dawning over time and was rather omitted in the previous chapters with the intent to provide stripped-down-to-essence listings. The type `U`, by the way, represents a not-otherwise-specified container component of an assumed widget toolkit. This is helpful to bridge to actual GUI implementations.

More related to the topic, the conversion of the `Item` interface to an abstract class may be based on experiences we've had with the initial strategy. Having only a `timeStamp` attribute is critical since there can be *different* items stamped with the *same* value. Tests verifying the behavior of scenarios with identical stamps uncover the subtleties. For example, fetching items page-wise requires the possibility of distinguishing items with the same timestamp value to avoid holes in the timeline entries.

Sufficient for the sample application, we've decided to go with an additional `id` attribute and defined a natural item order supplemented with appropriate equality checks, hence the `Comparable.compareTo(Item)`, `equals`, and `hashCode` implementations. This relieves subclasses and clients from handling these responsibilities.

 Note, however, that this also requires instances of a subtype of `Item` to be equal if their `id` attributes are equal.

Furthermore, the new `ItemUiMap` class catches the eye. It's a mediator between the timeline GUI and the model-managing component itself. As the name indicates, its purpose is to map `UiItem` entities to their underlying `Item` elements. This allows us to access an item's UI abstraction directly. It is useful to check its existence, refresh its relative timestamp designation, or perform top item calculations.

`ItemUiMap.fetch(FetchOperation)` delegates to the underlying model component to load either the next set of older items (`FetchOperation.MORE`) or the newly filed ones (`FetchOperation.NEW`). `ItemUiMap.update` avails the `UiItemFactory` reference to create `ItemUi` entities for items that have yet to be mapped or even call `ItemUI.update`. Overall, `ItemUiMap` abstracts the common UI functionality, which is independent from a certain widget toolkit. Consequently, it's possible to test the component with stubs specifying the generic type parameter `U` as `Object`.

Please note that the class diagram places `ItemUiMap` as a direct child of the timeline UI. This is a reduction to the essentials since a UI component itself is a composition based on several collaborators, with one of them actually referencing the map.

But architecture consists of more than a software's class structure. Because of this, let's discuss another related aspect with interesting insights from the book's point of view.

Separating concerns into modules

Recalling the introduction of the sample component's requirements, we remember that it has to run on different platforms (desktop, browser, and mobile) and allow the displaying of content from arbitrary sources. In other words, we expect the timeline component to be reusable by means of pluggable collaborators and from arbitrary widget toolkits.

Although it might be possible to realize this within a monolithic frame, such a strategy bears several disadvantages. Having all classes in one place is tempting, but it blurs the boundaries of higher-level building blocks. That's because it's all too easy to use a particular implementation detail of one block within another. This means they, sooner or later, blend in tightly coupled. As a result, changing a certain functionality most often affects more than a single block.

Additionally, providing all capabilities by a single archive usually increases the amount of references to third-party libraries. Just think about the various supported timeline UI platforms. Packaging the UI implementations together would be unfavorable since their dependencies would be induced transitively to every application incorporating our components even though most of them might not be needed at all.

But if they aren't needed, why bother? There is a reason to bother: third-party code might participate in initialization routines, wasting time and space without contributing any value. It may even happen that subject to the dependency resolution, they might conflict with diverging library versions required by other parts of the software. Using a wrong library version can cause difficult-to-track-down malfunctions. These kinds of problems are often referred to as *dependency hell*.

Hence, it seems reasonable to translate the argumentation of the single responsibility principle to more coarse-grained abstraction layers. Given that a coherent set of classes represents a higher-level concept, this *bundle* of classes should have only one reason to change with respect to the appropriate abstraction level. **Separation of concerns** means that we split up our components into different bundles, each of which is responsible for the realization of a certain concept. Bundles declare a usage API together with the necessary dependencies and can be deployed separately.

Distributing our classes into bundles of common responsibilities also reduces the dependency footprint. This is because an application only integrates those bundles that are actually needed for its particular purpose. Thus, a Swing UI wouldn't have any references to SWT. In general *separating the functionality of a program into independent, interchangeable bundles, such that each contains everything necessary to execute only one aspect of the desired functionality* is denoted as **modular programming**, *[MODPRO]*.

The following image shows how we can realize the sample requirements with several reusable bundles. At the top, we see application modules defining the executables for two of the supported platform environments. They depend on different widget toolkit-specific modules that supply the appropriate UI abstractions. But both environments share the same modules for the Git-related `Item` and `ItemProvider` implementations, the timeline core abstractions, and a utility module. The latter provides domain-unspecific helper classes applicable to all other modules.

With this structure in place, it's possible to extend the supported platforms without the need to change any of the existing modules. Based on the SWT timeline, for example, one can easily add another application module that serves as a browser and/or mobile backend (facilitated by the RAP/Tabris port of SWT, *[RAPRWT]*, *[TABRIS]*). This is because a deployable application is an assembly of a reasonable subset of modules.

Just as well one can provide an `ItemProvider` module based on REST services that connects to Twitter. After writing appropriate UI adapters for Swing Timeline, for example, you're able to integrate tweets regarding your favored hashtag into any Swing GUI-based application.

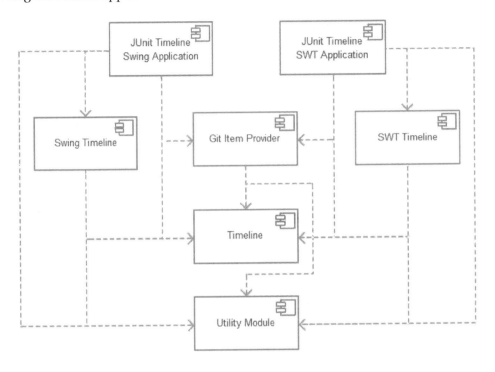

Module structure

Whether you're using a high-end modular environment, such as OSGi, Maven dependency management, or only plain old JARs. Thinking in terms of modules helps to separate your application into reusable building blocks, each of which serves a distinct purpose. This clarifies architectural responsibilities and confines deployment artifacts to the essential needs. In fact, modularity is considered so important that Project Jigsaw aims at providing it as a new language feature in Java 9, [JIGSAW].

But before discussing the effects of modules on the testing topic, let's look at another screenshot, which shows how modular development may look using one development project per module. As we use Maven throughout the sample application for dependency management, all modules have their own project object model file (`pom.xml`). A more detailed explanation of the POM's purpose follows in the next section. For brevity, this screenshot only shows Swing-related UI projects.

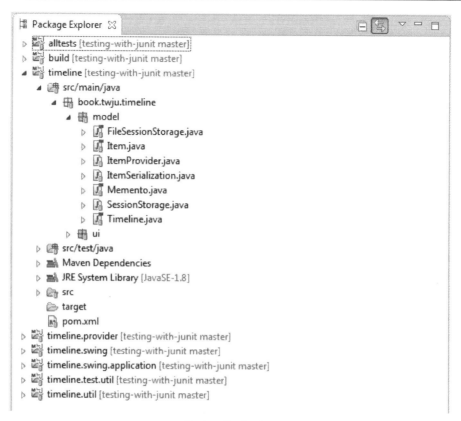

Project distribution

Noticeable at first glance is the `alltests` project, which doesn't seem to fit into the modularity context of this section. But working with modules hampers, a bit, the execution of all tests or specific subsets in a single launch from within the IDE. Using suites, as described in *Chapter 5, Using Runners for Particular Testing Purposes*, it's possible to specify several test sets with different granularity (unit, integration, or all) and put them in a test launch helper project. Vital for this approach to work is that the project has classpath dependencies on all the modules available in the IDE's workspace.

Next, we recognize the `build` project, which is responsible for compiling, verifying, and packaging our modules and/or applications. We'll supply a thorough description of the particulars in the subsequent section. For all others, we should be able to identify a match to an element of the previously shown module diagram; well, with one exception.

The `timeline.test.util` module serves only testing purposes and is not meant for application deployment at all. It contains test helper classes, which are useful for testing tasks of all (or most) of the modules under development. Thus, dependency declarations to this module are restricted to the test scope. Again, the followup section will bring more information on dependency and scope declarations. The following screenshot shows, among others, little helpers we've encountered throughout the book.

At this point, it's important to note that in a real-world software project, you might have several test helper modules. This is because test utilities may depend on certain functionality provided by other modules. Consider the `MementoAssert` helper from *Chapter 7, Improving Readability with Custom Assertions*, for example.

Test helper module

This class might be helpful with higher-level modules too. But to make it available for reuse, you have to unhinge it from the test source folder of the core timeline module. Putting it into `timeline.test.util` isn't a good idea since this would introduce a circular dependency. A clean solution supplies test helper classes for a certain module within a separate test utility module on an appropriate abstraction level.

At the close of the modularity explanations, let's have a look at the following image. This shows the result of supplementing the module structure shown previously with an RAP/Tabris executable module. Together with the screenshots of *Chapter 1, Getting Started*, showing the Swing, SWT, and Web Client variants, we are now able to happily declare mission accomplished.

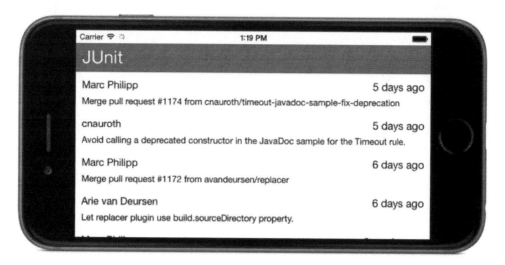

Timeline as a mobile application

After all the explanations on testing with JUnit, let's round up our workflow by giving a short introduction to a natural supplemental of test-driven development.

Setting up an automated CI build

JUnit tests are only valuable if they are executed regularly. This section explains the general purpose of continuous integration builds, which ascertains a high test execution frequency. Hence, CI constitutes a very good match to the *test first* approach.

What is continuous integration?

In *Chapter 1, Getting Started*, we mentioned the importance of immediate feedback with respect to unit testing. If we bust some low-level functionality, we want to know about it as soon as possible. This puts us in a position to detect and correct a problem as it evolves and avoid expensive quality assurance cycles. Because of this, it's good practice to run all tests at least once after merging and before checking in changes into **Version Control System (VCS)**. This reduces the risk of spoiling a teammate's day.

To give an impression, the following screenshot shows a test run of the complete test universe of the timeline sample:

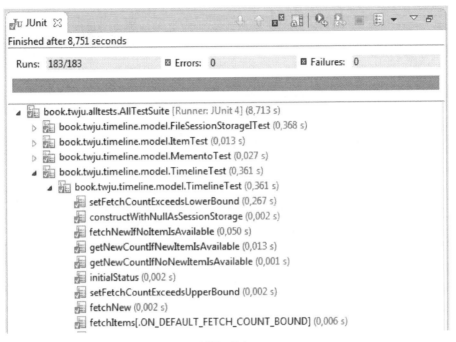

AllTestSuite

`AllTestSuite` includes unit and integration tests and took about 9 seconds to run. The problem is that on larger software projects, the execution time of this kind of suite can prolong up to several minutes. This makes running them manually on a regular basis a no-go. Nevertheless, you should run the unit tests locally as they are written to be fast!

But how can we achieve fast enough feedback at a reasonable price? An answer to that question is provided by **Continuous Integration** (**CI**). CI is a development practice where programmers check in their code changes to the shared main line of a VCS system several times a day. Each check-in gets verified by an automated build, providing reports and problem notifications. This allows us to detect merging deficiencies not only early enough, but also concurrently. The latter is important since, with CI, there is no blocking of the developer. They don't have to wait for the all test run to be completed successfully before they are allowed to do the actual check-in (blocking integration).

In a nutshell, CI supplements testing first with the following advantages:

- Detecting overall problems early and avoiding expensive QA circles
- Increasing the confidence building on a solid foundation
- Abolishing expensive and tense integration tasks
- Enabling us to deliver software more rapidly

The last point can be deduced directly from the fact that no more costly integration steps at the end of a development cycle are needed. Additionally, CI builds usually include the packaging of operative executables already. But before looking into the low-level details of a build setup, let's introduce the basic principles and practices of the approach.

Principles and practices

Fortunately, the benefits listed previously come at moderate costs. On the one hand, you need a VCS system, and on the other hand, you have to set up and maintain an automated build, which is usually the *first* thing to do when starting development work on a new project. In general, you should meet the following requirements:

- Maintaining a single-source code repository
- Automating the build
- Making your build self-testing
- Building every check-in on an integration machine
- Keeping the build fast
- Testing in a clone of the production environment
- Making it easy for anyone to get the latest executable
- Enabling everyone to see what's happening, *[CITHOU]*

Most of the bullet points should be self explanatory by now. But let's spend a few words on the less conclusive ones. Self-testing means that the build compiles the application modules and runs the unit tests against them. By running the tests in a clone of the production environment, the significance of successful completion gets amplified. In particular, this eliminates the *runs on my machine* problems. Finally, packaging the modules into an executable allows the product owner to inspect the operative application with the latest features at any time. This way, they can comment on functionality under development at very early stages.

To put CI into practice, developers participate in the following workflow:

- Developers check out code into their private workspaces
- When done, they check in their changes back to the repository
- The CI server monitors the repository and checks out changes when they occur
- The CI server builds the system and runs unit and integration tests
- The CI server releases deployable artifacts for testing
- The CI server assigns a build label to the version of the code it just built
- The CI server informs the team about the successful build
- If the build or tests fail, the CI server alerts the team
- The team fixes the issue at the earliest opportunity
- Continue to continually integrate and test throughout the project, *[CITHOU]*

There are several variants of this basic set of activities. A quite popular one, for example, integrates code review steps. This way, changes only get merged into the main line of development after several team members have signaled their OK.

 Note, however, that this also lowers the actual integration velocity.

Finally, for a successful CI adoption, there are responsibilities each team member has to accept:

- Check in frequently
- Don't check in broken code
- Don't check in untested code
- Don't check in when the build is broken
- Don't go home after checking in until the system builds, *[CITHOU]*

Again, most of the rules should be self explanatory given our initial remarks. You should avoid anything that weakens the significance of a successful build and take care to see that the runs stay unbroken. Failed integration impacts your teammates, which explains the importance of the last point. If you're not able to fix code that breaks a build immediately, you always have a chance to rewind to a previous revision and check in a fixed version of your latest changes the next day. With respect to the fourth rule, this means, of course, you are allowed to check in fixes to make a build succeed.

Failure notifications are usually done by e-mail but can be transmitted by other services too. To achieve optimum attention and keep the motivation high to fix broken builds fast, some teams additionally install so-called *extreme feedback devices*. These can be connected lava lamps, ambient orbs, or the like, within office rooms. Once such devices signal an alarm, everybody knows immediately that the build is in trouble and action has to be taken to get it back to normal.

The best way to digest all these preliminaries is to set up a build for our timeline sample.

Creating your own build

There are many tools that allow us to manage the build, report, and document tasks of a software under development. Without having preferences for a particular one, we've decided to go with Maven for this example just because of its widespread use. As already mentioned, the tool relies on the concept of **Project Object Model (POM)**. The model content gets defined by pom.xml files located usually in the root folders of the build-related source code projects.

To begin with, a project's POM contains basic information, such as the project's ID, version number, and packaging type. The ID comprises a common groupId shared, for example, by all timeline modules, and artifactId, identifying the individual modules of a group. The packaging element indicates the module's artifact type, such as JAR, WAR, EAR, and so on.

To build a compound of many modules, a so-called parent pom.xml is used. This model content contribution specifies our source code projects to build, declares common dependencies, and configures specific customizations. The following listing shows the head section of the sample's parent POM file located in our build project:

```
<project [...]>
  <modelVersion>4.0.0</modelVersion>

  <groupId>book.twju</groupId>
  <artifactId>build</artifactId>
  <version>0.0.1-SNAPSHOT</version>
  <packaging>pom</packaging>

  <properties>
    <project.build.sourceEncoding>
      UTF-8
```

```
      </project.build.sourceEncoding>
    </properties>

    <modules>
      <module>../timeline</module>
      <module>../timeline.swing</module>
      <module>../timeline.swing.application</module>
      <module>../timeline.provider</module>
      <module>../timeline.test.util</module>
      <module>../timeline.util</module>
      [...]
    </modules>

    [...]

  </project [...]>
```

As you can see, the terms module and (source code) project are used synonymously within this topic. Unfortunately, there is also the notion of the overall software project the build is related to. This can be a bit confusing at times but, hopefully, emerges from the context.

We continue with an excerpt of pom.xml residing in the timeline project, which demonstrates how modules refer back to their parent. By the way, the JAR packaging type is the default value and can be safely omitted:

```
<project [...]>
  <modelVersion>4.0.0</modelVersion>
  <artifactId>timeline</artifactId>
  <packaging>jar</packaging>

  <parent>
    <groupId>book.twju</groupId>
    <artifactId>build</artifactId>
    <version>0.0.1-SNAPSHOT</version>
    <relativePath>../build/pom.xml</relativePath>
  </parent>

  [...]

</project>
```

Each POM can declare dependencies to third-party libraries needed for compilation and/or execution. The tool's runtime resolves them by loading the appropriate artifacts from a central repository server by default. Then, they get stored in a local repository on the disk for subsequent requests. Of course, which remote repositories to query is customizable.

In addition, the local repository can be populated with artifacts created by local builds. In our example, this would be the timeline module archives. The next snippet illustrates how dependency declarations look:

```
<dependencies>
  <dependency>
    <groupId>junit</groupId>
    <artifactId>junit</artifactId>
    <version>4.12</version>
    <scope>test</scope>
  </dependency>
</dependencies>
```

Please note the `scope` tag. Without going into detail, running a Maven build requires us to specify a certain goal to be met. Executing a POM with the goal *test*, for example, means to go through the validate, compile, and test phase of the tool's processing life cycle. The `scope` tag value *test* means that a referenced library gets added to the classpath during test case compilations and test executions only. Consequently, these dependencies will not be available in the course of the compile phase. In general, `scope` limits the transitivity of a dependency and is biased with the classpath used for various build tasks.

> Note that it's possible to declare dependencies needed by more than one module at the parent POM level.

Build customizations are done by adding or reconfiguring so-called plugins. As the name indicates, they make it possible to extend the available capabilities by embedding specific artifacts. The following excerpt of the parent `pom.xml` configures, for example, the Java compiler to allow JDK 8 sources:

```
<build>
  <plugins>
    <plugin>
      <groupId>org.apache.maven.plugins</groupId>
      <artifactId>maven-compiler-plugin</artifactId>
      <version>3.3</version>
      <configuration>
```

```
      <source>1.8</source>
      <target>1.8</target>
    </configuration>
  </plugin>
 </plugins>
</build>
```

Once we're done with our build definition, the last thing to do is launch it. The next command-line instruction shows, for example, how to invoke the Maven executable `mvn` with the goals `clean` and `test`. Hereby, we assume the working directory points to the location of the parent `pom.xml`. The clean life cycle removes all files generated by the previous build and gets executed first. Afterwards, the default life cycle compiles the modules from scratch and runs them against the available tests. Test result reports are written to the console:

```
mvn clean test
```

With the Maven build in place, we've set up the CI requirement of a self-checking, automated build. But where do we get our integration machine from, and how do we register our build definition with it? Luckily, there are a lot of offers that facilitate this task. If you tend to host an integration machine by yourself, you may resort to one of the integration server applications, such as Jenkins CI, *[JENKIN]*, TeamCity, *[TEACIT]*, and so on.

But the cool kids nowadays employ Cloud CI services that use integration hooks into source code repository providers, such as GitHub, out of the box. This makes it only a minor configuration effort to get your integration machine up and running as soon as your automated build configuration works. Examples of such service vendors are Travis, *[TRAVIS]*, Codeship, *[CODSHI]*, and Cloudbees, *[CLOBEE]*.

One of the nice things about using GitHub combined with Travis or Codeship is that usage is free for public projects. Hence, we host the sources of our sample application at GitHub (`https://github.com/fappel/Testing-with-JUnit`) and let the automated builds be performed by Travis. All we need to do is log in at Travis with our GitHub account, activate our source code repository to build, and add a configuration file (`.travis.yml`) to the root directory of our source code repository. This file specifies which JVM to use, sets the build command-line instructions, defines `after-success` steps, and the like. The following snippet gives an impression of how such a configuration may look:

```
language: java
jdk:
  - oraclejdk8
branches:
```

```
only:
   - master
script: mvn -f sample.application/build/pom.xml clean verify
```

Believe it or not, that's it, and from now on, every new commit will trigger a build execution (for configuration details, refer to the Travis online documentation).

The following screenshot shows the correlation between the sample application's source code repository and the tied integration build service. The vertical green bar indicates that the build of the latest commit has finished successfully. In the event of a failure, the bar would be drawn in red.

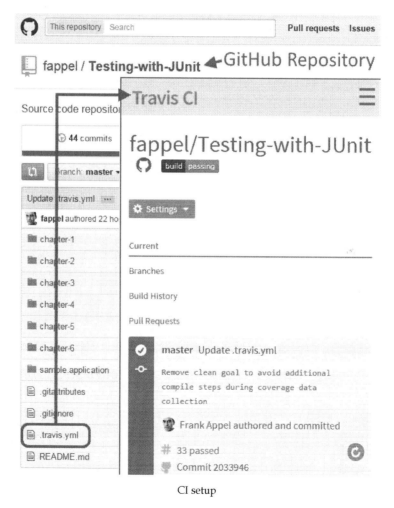

CI setup

With the CI build working, it's possible to add various quality measurement reports. Representatively, we'll have a look at how this can be done with code coverage.

Integrating code coverage reports

The last section will revisit and deepen the knowledge about the assets and drawbacks of code coverage. It'll conclude this book by showing you how to add coverage analysis to your CI build.

Enlarging on code coverage

Recall *Chapter 2, Writing Well-structured Tests*, and we know code coverage reports can be a useful tool to detect gaps of untested passages in our production classes. However, full coverage does not guarantee complete or even reasonable behavior verification. To substantiate these statements a bit more, let's take a look at a class highlighted with full coverage:

```java
 7  public class MouseHandler {
 8
 9    private boolean mouseDown;
10
11    public boolean isMouseDown() {
12      return mouseDown;
13    }
14
15    public void markMouseDown() {
16      mouseDown = true;
17    }
18
19    public void handleMouseUp( MouseEvent event, Runnable runnable ) {
20      if( mouseDown && inRange( event ) ) {
21        runnable.run();
22      }
23      mouseDown = false;          Branch Coverage Markers
24    }
25
26    private static boolean inRange( MouseEvent event ) {
27      Point size = ( ( Control )event.widget).getSize();
28      return event.x >= 0 && event.x <= size.x && event.y >= 0 && event.y <= size.y;
29    }
30  }
```

Full coverage

The preceding image shows the alleged pleasant case if full instruction and branch coverage has been reached. But it can't be stressed enough that full coverage alone testifies nothing about the quality of the underlying assertions!

The only reasonable conclusion to draw is that there are obviously no uncovered spots. In this sense, adding a single statement to a covered path of execution, for example, can alter the overall outcome of a test's exercise phase and still pass its existing verifications.

If we, however, get a result such as in the following screenshot, we are in trouble for sure. As you can see, the tests do not cover several branches and miss an instruction entirely. This means there is still work to do. The obvious solution seems to be to add a few tests to close these gaps.

> "If a part of your test suite is weak in a way that coverage can detect, it's likely also weak in a way coverage can't detect."

> – Brian Marik

Considering the preceding quote and the reflections, coverage holes may very well be an indication of a more fundamental problem. The difficulty with code coverage is that it cannot detect missing code that *ought* to be there but isn't. Marik describes such faults of omission as *code not complex enough for the problem, [MARI]*. In other words, coverage can't tell us about missing code on boundary conditions and corner cases that we haven't anticipated. Because of this, it's advisable to reconsider gap-affected scenarios thoroughly:

Missed instructions and branches

Before showing you how to integrate coverage reporting into our Maven build, we once again advice you that full coverage is not always achievable or can be unreasonably expensive to achieve. So, be careful not to overdo things.

Automating reporting

Coverage report data is collected at the time of execution of a software. To enable reporting, the software's classes need to be instrumented by a special tool. In our case, we use Jacoco, *[JACOCO]*, as it supports Java 8. Maven integration is provided by an additional plugin, which takes care to instrument classes before test runs and stores the reported data to the disk. The following excerpt of the parent pom. xml shows the base inclusion. The full configuration details can be inspected in the sample's source code repository:

```
<plugin>
  <groupId>org.jacoco</groupId>
  <artifactId>jacoco-maven-plugin</artifactId>
  <version>0.7.4.201502262128</version>
  <executions>
    [...]
  /executions>
</plugin>
```

While our build is capable of producing reports, the last thing to do is to visualize and make them available for team members and other interested parties. Luckily, there are online coverage reporting services available. One of them is Coveralls, *[COVALL]*, that integrates seamlessly with GitHub and that is free for public repositories. All we have to do is add a Coverall Maven plugin reference, *[TRAUTO]*, to our parent POM and introduce an after-success step to our .travis.yml configuration file. The following snippet shows how to trigger coverage data recording and report uploading to Coveralls from Travis:

```
after_success:
  - mvn -f sample.application/build/pom.xml test \
    jacoco:report coveralls:report
```

The following screenshot shows an excerpt of the coverage history and the statistics of the latest build of our sample application at the time of writing this:

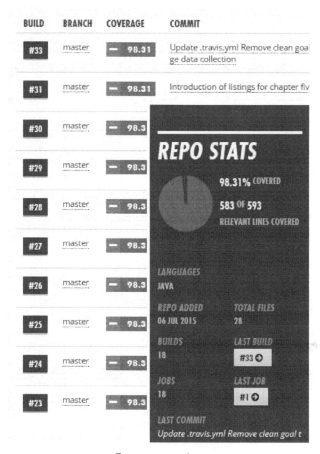

Coverage overview

Of course, it is possible to drill down to the hotspots and see in highlighted code viewers what branches and instructions have been missed (see the following screenshot). The private `Iterables` constructor is an example of a coverage gap that would be unreasonably expensive to close. Thus, we won't get any sleepless nights about it.

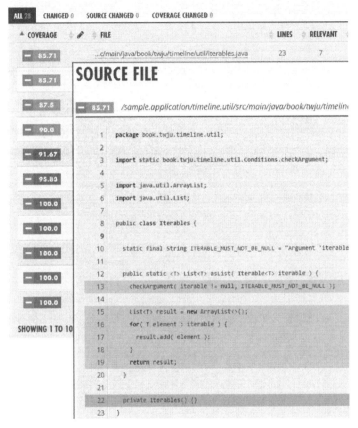

File drill down

Naturally, it's possible to configure threshold values and notifications to, for example, alarm team members immediately about falling below an expected minimum coverage. This alarm system is a valuable contribution to the early feedback system we maintain by writing our tests first and using continuous integration.

Now, before concluding the book, and after going through the references used, let's recap for a last time what you learned in this chapter.

Summary

In the last chapter, we concluded the example application by refining the timeline's class design. You learned about important test-related architectural aspects of modularization and reusable test helper classes. Furthermore, you got to know that continuous integration supplements the *test first* approach very well by automatically running tests after each check-in of changes to the VCS. Applying these insights, you experienced what it takes to set up a CI build for the book's sample. Last but not least, you deepened your knowledge on code coverage and incorporated a reporting tool into your CI system.

Arriving at the end of this book, you gained a good perception of the conceptual requirements, a wide-ranging arsenal of solution approaches, and the premises to master the daily-work challenges of testing with JUnit. But remember that skill comes with practice and life's not easy at the bottom; in particular, when starting within a legacy system at hand, which lacks any tests until the time you start work on it.

In that case, begin with a CI build and a few islands of tests for components written to solve your actual development tasks. Ensure that these new components are tested under proper isolation from third-party vendor libraries *and* your old code if it's expensive to use. Continue to grow the islands with every new requirement and carefully rework legacy code that comes in the way. But avoid touching running passages for no reason.

 For more details on how to deal with legacy code, you can refer to *Working Effectively with Legacy Code* by Michael C. Feathers, *[FEAT05]*.

Continuously following this practice over time, the islands will grow, mass together, and finally form prospering continents providing large areas of well-tested and properly written code. So be patient—it won't come overnight but will definitely be worth the effort.

References

Chapter 1

- **[BECK03]**: Beck. *Test-Driven Development: By Example*. Pearson Education, Inc. 2003.
- **[FOWL06]**: Fowler. *Xunit*. http://www.martinfowler.com/bliki/Xunit.html. 2006.
- **[FUTU99]**: Futurama. *Space Pilot 3000*. 1999.
- **[HUTH03]**: Hunt and Thomas. *The Pragmatic Programmer*. LLC. 2004.
- **[MESZ07]**: Meszaros. *xUnit Test Patterns: Refactoring Test Code*. Pearson Education, Inc. 2007.
- **[TECDEP]**: Wikipedia. *Technical debt*. https://en.wikipedia.org/wiki/Technical_debt.

Chapter 2

- **[BECK03]**: Beck. *Test-Driven Development: By Example*. Pearson Education, Inc. 2003.
- **[FOWL2H]**: Fowler. http://martinfowler.com/bliki/TwoHardThings.html.
- **[FOWL12]**: Fowler. http://martinfowler.com/bliki/TestCoverage.html. 2012.
- **[FOWL13]**: Fowler. http://martinfowler.com/bliki/GivenWhenThen.html. 2013.
- **[HUTH03]**: Hunt and Thomas. *The Pragmatic Programmer*. LLC. 2004.

- **[JBEHAV]**: *JBehave*. http://jbehave.org/.
- **[KACZ13]**: Kaczanowski. *Practical Unit Testing with JUnit and Mockito*. 2013.
- **[MARI]**: Marick. http://www.exampler.com/testing-com/writings/coverage.pdf.
- **[MART09]**: Martin. *Clean Code*. Pearson Education, Inc. 2008.
- **[MESZ07]**: Meszaros. *xUnit Test Patterns: Refactoring Test Code*. Pearson Education, Inc. 2007.
- **[NORT06]**: North. *Introducing BDD*. http://dannorth.net/introducing-bdd/. 2006.
- **[OSHE05]**: Osherove. http://osherove.com/blog/2005/4/3/naming-standards-for-unit-tests.html. 2005.
- **[SHOR04]**: Shore. http://www.martinfowler.com/ieeeSoftware/failFast.pdf. 2004.

Chapter 3

- **[APPE14]**: Appel. *Clean SWT Listener Notifications with SWTEventHelper*. http://www.codeaffine.com/2014/03/10/clean-swt-listener-notifcations-with-swteventhelper/. 2014.
- **[BOLD11]**: Boldischar. *Mocking Frameworks Considered Harmful*, http://www.disgruntledrats.com/?p=620. 2011.
- **[EASYMO]**: *EasyMock*. http://easymock.org/.
- **[FRPR10]**: Freeman and Pryce. *Growing Object-Oriented Software, Guided by Tests*. Addison-Wesley. 2010.
- **[MIVIPR]**: Wikipedia. *Minimal viable product*. https://en.wikipedia.org/wiki/Minimum_viable_product.
- **[FOWL04]**: Fowler. *Inversion of Control Containers and the Dependency Injection pattern*. http://martinfowler.com/articles/injection.html. 2004.
- **[FOWL05]**: Fowler. *FluentInterface*. http://martinfowler.com/bliki/FluentInterface.html. 2005.
- **[GOUL12]**: Goulding. *Test Double Terminology*. http://jakegoulding.com/blog/2012/01/12/test-double-terminology/. 2012.
- **[JMOCK]** : *jMock*. http://www.jmock.org/.
- **[KACZ13]**: Kaczanowski. *Practical Unit Testing with JUnit and Mockito*. 2013.
- **[MART02]**: Martin. *Agile Software Development: Principles, Patterns, and Practices*. Prentice Hall. 2002.

- **[MART14]**: Martin. *When to Mock.* http://blog.8thlight.com/uncle-bob/2014/05/10/WhenToMock.html. 2014.

- **[MESZ07]**: Meszaros. *xUnit Test Patterns: Refactoring Test Code.* Pearson Education, Inc. 2007.

- **[SOELPR]**: Wikipedia. *Somebody else's problem.* https://en.wikipedia.org/wiki/Somebody_else%27s_problem.

- **[MOCKIT]**: *Mockito.* http://mockito.org/.

- **[PRIM13]**: Primat. *GitHub's 10,000 most Popular Java Projects – Here are The Top Libraries They Use,* http://blog.takipi.com/githubs-10000-most-popular-java-projects-here-are-the-top-libraries-they-use/. 2013.

- **[SWT]**: *SWT: The Standard Widget Toolkit,* https://www.eclipse.org/swt/.

- **[TRAWRE]**: *Train Wreck.* http://c2.com/cgi/wiki?TrainWreck. 2014.

- **[WIKILD]**: Wikipedia. *Law of Demeter.* http://en.wikipedia.org/wiki/Law_of_Demeter.

Chapter 4

- **[FISBOW]**: Fishbowl. http://stefanbirkner.github.io/fishbowl/index.html.

- **[HEVEEC]**: Hejlsberg, Venners, and Eckel. *The Trouble with Checked Exceptions.* http://www.artima.com/intv/handcuffs.html. 2003.

- **[SHOR04]**: Shore. *Fail Fast.* http://www.martinfowler.com/ieeeSoftware/failFast.pdf. 2004.

Chapter 5

- **[BURST]** : *Burst.* https://github.com/square/burst.

- **[CPSUIT]**: *ClasspathSuite.* https://github.com/takari/takari-cpsuite.

- **[JUNITP]**: *JUnitParams.* http://pragmatists.github.io/JUnitParams.

- **[OSGIAL]**: *OSGi.* http://www.osgi.org/Technology/HomePage.

- **[OSGITE]**: *Automated OSGi Test Suite.* https://github.com/rherrmann/osgi-testsuite.

Chapter 6

- **[ASPECT]**: *AspectJ*. `https://eclipse.org/aspectj/`.

- **[FOWL11]**: Fowler. *Eradicating Non-Determinism in Tests*. `http://martinfowler.com/articles/nonDeterminism.html#Quarantine`. 2011.

- **[HERR13]**: Herrman. *A JUnit Rule to Conditionally Ignore Tests*. `http://www.codeaffine.com/2013/11/18/a-junit-rule-to-conditionally-ignore-tests/`. 2013.

- **[SYSRUL]**: *System Rules*. `http://stefanbirkner.github.io/system-rules/`.

Chapter 7

- **[ASSJAD]**: *Class Assert*. `http://junit.org/javadoc/latest/org/junit/Assert.html`.

- **[ASSERJ]**: *AssertJ*. `http://joel-costigliola.github.io/assertj/`.

- **[GHJV96]**: Gamma, Helm, Johnson, and Vlissides. *An Introduction to Design Patterns*. Addison-Wesley. 1996.

- **[HAMJAV]**: *JavaHamcrest*. `https://github.com/hamcrest/JavaHamcrest`.

- **[OPECLO]**: *Open/closed principle*. `https://en.wikipedia.org/wiki/Open/closed_principle`.

- **[UTAS14]**: Comment by David M. Karr. `http://www.codeaffine.com/2014/09/10/junit-nutshell-unit-test-assertions/`.

Chapter 8

- **[CITHOU]**: *Continuous Integration*. `http://www.thoughtworks.com/de/continuous-integration`. ThoughtWorks.

- **[CLOBEE]**: *CloudBees*. `https://www.cloudbees.com/`.

- **[CODSHI]**: *Codeship*. `https://codeship.com/`.

- **[COVALL]**: *Coveralls*. `https://coveralls.io/`.

- **[FEAT05]**: Feathers. *Working Effectively with Legacy Code*. Pearson Education, Inc. 2005.

- **[JENKIN]**: *Jenkins*. `https://jenkins-ci.org/`.

- **[JACOCO]**: *JaCoCo*. `http://www.eclemma.org/jacoco/`.

- **[JIGSAW]**: *Jigsaw Quick Start*. `http://openjdk.java.net/projects/jigsaw/doc/quickstart.html`.

- **[MARI]** : Marick. *How to Misuse Code Coverage.* `http://www.exampler.com/testing-com/writings/coverage.pdf`.

- **[MODPRO]**: *Modular programming.* `https://en.wikipedia.org/wiki/Modular_programming`.

- **[RAPRWT]**: *RAP.* `http://www.eclipse.org/rap/`.

- **[TABRIS]**: *Tabris.* `http://developer.eclipsesource.com/tabris/`.

- **[TEACIT]**: *TeamCity.* `https://www.jetbrains.com/teamcity/`.

- **[TRAUTO]**: *coveralls-maven-plugin.* `https://github.com/trautonen/coveralls-maven-plugin`.

- **[TRAVIS]**: *Travis CI.* `https://travis-ci.org/`.